the

Dance

House

Lakota Fancy Dancer #2, Rosebud Reservation, July 1991
Palladium Print by David Michael Kennedy

the
Dance
House

STORIES FROM ROSEBUD

by Joseph Marshall III

MUSEUM OF NEW MEXICO PRESS
SANTA FE

10 9 8 7 6 5 4 3 2 1 (Museum of New Mexico Press PB edition)

Manufactured in the United States of America
Cover photograph by David Michael Kennedy
Book design by Beverly Miller Atwater

Library of Congress Cataloging-in-Publication Data

Marshall, Joe.
  The dance house : stories from Rosebud / Joseph Marshall III.
    p.   cm.
  Contents: Oliver's silver dollar—Cozy by the fire—Nelson and Star—The
1963 Continental—The dance house—When the grasses talk—Pride—The birthday
turtle—the bloodlines of heritage—The myth of the hunter warrior—Buffalo grass—
White love—Lure of the Holy iron.
  ISBN 978-089013-526-6 (pbk.: alk. Paper)
  1. Rosebud Indian Reservation (S.D.)—Social life and customs—Fiction.
2. Indians of North America—South Dakota—Fiction. 3. Teton Indians—
Fictionm.   1. Title
PS3563.A7221SD36   1998
813' .54—DC21   98-20752
                                                                      CIP

Museum of New Mexico Press
P.O. Box 2087
Santa Fe, New Mexico 87504
www.mnmpress.org

Table of Contents

Foreword

▲   Henry Luce—with Briton Hadden founders of TIME—
▲   was a proponent of "The Great Man" theory of history, a
▲   belief that individuals, more than collective forces of
▲   society, determine the course of human events.
▲   Because this is the United States of America, there *is*
an American Diversity, an American Identity and there
are those who have defined the American Experience,
and the tradition will continue through generations to
come.

Of those influences, and perhaps foremost, are the
stories told by Indian Voices: the artist Edgar Heap of
Birds (Oklahoma), the dramatist Lynn Riggs (Cherokee
Nation), the dance of Maria Tallchief (Osage), novelist
and politician Christine Quintasket (Interior Salish), the
long fiction of N. Scott Momaday (Kiowa/Cherokee), the
poetry of Linda Hogan (Chickasaw Nation), and Joseph
Marshall III.

The pages of *The Dance House* are not crammed with words, but,
rather, have been printed sparingly. Marshall moves slowly,
steadily, unrelentingly toward a harmony so subtle as to be
almost incomprehensible. In communicating the legends and
myths of the Sicangu Lakota, he writes reverently of the land and
all who have passed through it. His aim is to communicate in a
literary form, alien to the stories his people created. Joseph

Marshall passes them on without diminishing their authenticity. His writings focus on how Native Americans relate to contemporary society without denying their ancient language. Capturing peoples he has known, entwining their foibles, weaknesses, and strengths, conversations and wisdom, Marshall's poetic gifts surface whenever the beauty of the natural world is invoked.

It is unfair, I believe, to compare authors, past and present, anymore than I think it is fair to single out individuals who have or will influence history, against the maelstrom of superficial society. However, Joseph Marshall III in terms of content and reception has made Native American life less marginalized and isolated. *The Dance House* takes its place among the first literatures of the United States.

—Michael Evans Smith
The Bloomsbury Review

Introduction

▲   Joseph Marshall's powerful first novel, *Winter of the Holy*
▲   *Iron*, was published in 1994. I was already aware of
▲   Marshall's work as an educator and historian. He was a
▲   co-founder of Sinte Gleska University in Rosebud, South
▲   Dakota and co-author of *Soldiers Falling Into Camp*, a
groundbreaking history that told the story of the Indian
victory against the forces of George Armstrong Custer
from the point of view of the Native people, Absaroke
and Lakota, who fought on both sides.

Winter of the Holy Iron was something entirely different. Its
accomplishment was breathtaking. Not only did it deal with the
time of changes for his Sicangu Lakota people that came with
the arrival of white men and their firearms, it also delved into
the complex moral issues about the place of the warrior in a traditional culture and the use of that powerful weapon the Lakota
named *maza wakan*, the "mysterious, holy iron." It ends with the
main character making a vow to his people that he "will always
go to the hunt or ride the warpath with the lance, and the bow
and arrows." For him, the sound of the rifle would always be:

> "...a new voice, not of the land. It was the
> voice of a stranger. One that would speak more
> and more. For Whirlwind, it would always bring
> memories of the first time he ever heard it. For
> him, it would always be the voice of death."

Since *Winter of the Holy Iron,* I've have held the greatest admiration for the work of Joseph Marshall. His second book, a collection of essays entitled *On Behalf of the Wolf and the First Peoples* deepened my regard. Its blend of history, vision, and personal experience is striking. Every chapter is as bright as the light of the morning star. Looking again at that book and the essay entitled "On Making a Bow," I recall the thought I had when I first read it—if Henry David Thoreau had been born in this century as a Sicangu Lakota, this is the sort of writing he might have done. I consider Joseph Marshall to be one of the finest contemporary writers of the English language. He represents an indigenous, ethnic, and cultural heritage with skill, intelligence, careful honesty, and measured pride. He writes with a graceful clarity that is often pure poetry to read. His work is an important contribution to both American literature and World literature.

I believe that the best authors do not have to write about everything to be universal. Instead, they must know something, know it as well as they know their own breath. It does not matter how small that focus may be. It might be a hill in the Kiowa country of Oklahoma called Rainy Mountain. Or it might be three small green circles in the spring grass of the Little White River Valley in South Dakota. And then they must write about it in a way that enables the reader to see what they see, to share the emotion and the experience.

The Dance House has deepened my appreciation of Joseph Marshall's work even further. I find myself alternately moved and instructed by these stories which flow from essay to autobiography to storytelling, sometimes combining all three. And I find myself wanting to just plain go out and tell everyone I see to read this book.

I hope they will, though I fear that many who like reading about Indians will find parts of this book perplexing. Ironically, as Marshall himself points out in "The Myth of the Hunter/Warrior" and "White Lore," non-indigenous Americans are fascinated by Indians, but the Indian of popular American imagination is largely just that—imaginary! And the most popular of Indians are the warbonneted Sioux, Marshall's own Lakota people. To be even more precise, Marshall's people are the Sicangu Lakota.

One problem is that the real truth about Native American cultures and the recent referring to the last 500 years—a brief span of time considering the many generations before the intruders—histories of the more than four hundred North American Native tribal nations are often hard for non-Natives to believe. American audiences will swallow whole the improbable scenario in a movie such as *Dances With Wolves* of a shell-shocked white soldier coming into a Lakota village, becoming a trusted leader overnight and even finding buffalo when the poor Indians cannot. (One Lakota friend of mine tells me that B.C. out in South Dakota used to mean before Custer to the Lakotas, but now it means before Costner.)

Yet when you tell those same credulous people that the Indian Health Service was sterilizing Native American women without their consent less than twenty years ago or that radioactive tailings from the uranium mines in New Mexico were knowingly dumped in Pueblo villages, they cannot believe it. At times, it seems as if a day hardly goes by without my having someone respond to an absolutely verifiable statement about Native people with incredulity.

But telling the truth was and remains highly regarded among the indigenous peoples of this continent. So much so that often when a man sat down to tell a story about his experiences—as did the Oglala Lakota holy man Black Elk in *Black Elk Speaks*—he would make sure to have at least one other person present who had witnessed those experiences to vouch for their veracity. Like Black Elk, Joseph Marshall respects the truth and tells it.

With that in mind, here are some corroborating facts that vouch for the frequently poignant truths told by Joseph Marshall's stories in this book.

The first story, "Oliver's Silver Dollar" may seem farfetched to some. Could a Lakota man really be put into a state mental institution because of a linguistic or cultural misunderstanding? Can one social worker have that much effect on a Native person's life?

A joke that has been around for some years in Indian country is that the family structure has changed drastically since the coming of white culture. In the old days, an Indian family in most places consisted of a father, a mother, their children, one or more sets of grandparents and various uncles, aunts and cousins. Nowadays, Indian families are much larger. They consist of a father, a mother, their children, one or more sets of grandparents, various uncles, aunts and cousins, an anthropologist, a social worker and a documentary film maker.

Some years ago, I was one of a number of writers, artists and storytellers invited to take part in the centennial of Haskell Institute, the famous, or infamous, Indian Boarding School in Kansas. In recent years, Haskell has shifted from being an assimilationist institution dedicated to the teaching of white ways to Native students, into an Indian-run Junior College sensitive to the cultures of indigenous Americans. A group of us were talking about the old graveyard at Haskell. Every Indian school had such a graveyard. Far too many of the children who were taken from the warmth of loving families to the coldness of the boarding school succumbed to disease shortly after arriving at places like Haskell. Some perished as a result of the epidemics that swept with regularity through all the Indian boarding schools. Some died, literally, of broken hearts.

"Did you ever hear about the Indian Insane Asylum?" someone said.

"I didn't know there was one," I answered, hoping that the person was joking. But she wasn't.

"There was," she said. "I'm working on a paper about it. It seems that someone in the United States Government decided that an Insane Asylum for Indians would be a good idea. So they built one, a nice big new building that could hold hundreds of insane Indians. Then they sent word out to all the Superintendents, asking them to send all their insane Indians. Months went by without a reply. Finally they asked the Superintendents, 'Where are your insane Indians?' And do you know what all the Superindents said?"

"We don't have any?"

"That's right, that is just what they said. So, can you guess what the government said back to those Superintendents?"

"Find some."

"And so they did. They picked out people they regarded as troublemakers on the reservations, people who didn't do what they were told or tried to hold to tradition. And they were able to fill up that insane asylum for Indians."

We stood there for a few seconds without saying anything. Then a Lakota hoop dancer and flute player who was standing beside me, broke the silence. "My Uncle," he said, "was one of those troublemakers sent to that insane asylum. He died there."

And what about a tale such as the title story "The Dance House," where a group of traditional old men find a way around the government's decree against dancing? Was the United States government that petty and ethnocentric?

On February 14, 1923, Charles H. Burke, the United States Commissioner of Indian Affairs addressed a document to the Area Superintendents of the Bureau of Indian Affairs. Identified as *Indian Dancing: Supplement to Circular No. 1665*, it included a number of recommendations that had been adopted at a conference of Christian missionaries in the Sioux country. Prominent among those recommendations were the following:

1. That the Indian form of gambling and lottery known as the *ituranpi*, "give away" be prohibited.

2. That the Indian dances be limited to one each month in the daylight hours of one day in the midweek, and at one center in each district; the months of March and April, June, July and August be excepted.

3. That none take part in the dances, or be present who are under 50 years of age.

4. That a careful propaganda be undertaken to educate public opinion against the dance and to provide a healthy substitute.

The purpose of these restrictions, Commissioner Burke explained, was for the "best welfare" of the Indian, a means of preventing "idleness, waste of time of whatever nature, and the neglect of physical resources upon which depend food, clothing, shelter, and the very beginning of progress." A rather large book could be filled with a collection of such government directives issued over a period of more than half a century, all designed to, as Marshall rightly states "kill the Indian and save the man."

It takes tough people to tell tough truths. The place on this earth that the Sicangu Lakota people call home is a place that either makes you tough or kills you. South Dakota is as much a state of mind as it is a state of the union. In the old days one's age was not measured by how many years a person lived, but by how many winters a person survived.

One February I was invited to South Dakota to do poetry readings. Knowing that South Dakota was notorious for the severity of its winters, I accepted. I checked into a hotel room for the night and was wakened in my colder than expected ground floor room near dawn by the sound of someone or something whistling. I went to the window to look out, but I could not. Seven feet of snow had drifted over the top of the windows and doors. The whistling blizzard wind was still piling on more. I was stuck in that motel for two days and it gave me new respect for the power of nature on the plains, a place where there are frequently greater extremes of temperature within a twenty-four hour period, from eighty above zero to fifty below, than anywhere else on the entire planet.

So, when I read the two stories in this new book that deal with the living presence of the winter storm—"Cozy By The Fire" and "Nelson and Star," I had a very real appreciation for the experience of winter survival that is a central element in both tales.

All of the stories that you are about to read are worthy of praise and discussion. I recommend reading them one at a time. Give yourself the time to sit and think, preferably somewhere outside, where you can look up into the sky in the hope of seeing an eagle's widespread wings. Let each story sink in before moving on to the next one. Each of them will say more to you than I can.

One story in this collection, the story called "Pride," should be put into every collection of the year's best stories and made required reading in our high schools. I urge a Native filmmaker with intelligence and stubborn integrity to turn it into a movie. I haven't mentioned until now the affinity for horses that glows from the pages of this book, but "Pride" is one of the most moving and painfully felt stories I've ever read about horses and Native people. It is about a boy's memories, about the old Lakota way of gentling a horse, about the pride of men, the heart of a half-blind paint named Rock, about "the connection to a past when life and glory depended on the courage of such a horse."

It is a good way to end, thinking about such a story.

—Joseph Bruchac

Oliver's Silver Dollar

▲   Oliver Snow Bear came home to the reservation in 1967
▲   after thirty years in the State Mental Hospital. Those who
▲   knew him best will tell you that his sanity was never in
▲   question. Thirty years of his life was spent behind cold
▲   brick walls and an eight-foot-high fence because of his
choice of words. But if Oliver's choice of words is to be
called into question, what about the judgment of the
person who acted on those words?

Oliver's mother and father died in the Spanish
influenza epidemic that swept across the reservation in
1919. That year he was five and sole heir to 320 acres of
prime bottomland.

For the next thirteen years, he lived in two house-
holds. His mother's first cousin, Effie Grass Lodge, took
him in until he was twelve. But when her husband, who
worked for the railroad, was killed in a train accident
Oliver left to ease the burden on Effie's meager means.
During the following few years, Oliver attended a Catholic
boarding school. Though he was an apt student, his verbal skills
in English far surpassed his ability to read and write the language. He struggled with written English whenever he encoun-
tered it.

After a year at boarding school, Oliver was signed out for the
summer by the First Chargers, a large family who couldn't resist

adding one more. The summer arrangement turned into a five-year commitment, until Oliver turned eighteen. The day after his eighteenth birthday Oliver succumbed to the wanderlust deep in the blood. The Sicangu Lakota, after all, had been nomadic hunters, and genetic memory could not be erased in two generations. He left all but $5 of the $72 he had managed to earn and save in a jar on the First Chargers' doorstep, along with a note which simply said *"Pilamayapelo,"* or "You have made me grateful."

For the next five years, Oliver wandered over the entire reservation. It was an adventure, to be sure. He was often alone, which was understandable. Not only was he a loner, but his chosen lifestyle separated him from the usual haunts of people—the trading posts, churches, the Bureau of Indian Affairs issue stations, and the temporary Indian settlements that appeared here and there across the reservation.

Though he was six feet tall, Oliver was not a big man. There was a friendly glimmer in his brown eyes, and his wide mouth always seemed to be on the verge of a smile. A long, narrow nose gave him an air of dignity, but his coarse, unbound hair hanging below his shoulders made him look a little wild. Years of living outdoors had given him a weathered, leathery appearance, and anyone seeing him for the first time guessed that he was far older than he really was.

Oliver cared little for some of the new things that many Lakota people found exciting: a new religion, automobiles, radios, rock candy, the Fourth of July, and Christmas. Since he lived life on an elemental level he was more impressed with the practical things that were part of the white man's culture, such as iron tools, window glass, and field glasses. However, he had no use for clocks, feeling that sunrise, sunset, the sun in the middle of the sky, and night were all the indicators of time he would ever need. Calendars were about as useful as clocks, as far as Oliver was concerned. After all, the seasons came and went with obvious changes which didn't need verification from lines, squares, and numbers on a page.

Because of his nomadic lifestyle, Oliver reasoned that if he lived like the whites it would be impossible for him to carry all the things he would need just to get by. Therefore, at any given time Oliver only carried two changes of clothes, two bars of soap, food enough for two days, a water flask, a good knife, various lengths of rope, and two woolen blankets. With these things he could survive with comfort and still travel fast.

Oliver was a hunter and fisherman. Many a rabbit or squirrel was caught in his snares or fell to a well-placed stone from a leather sling. He was especially fond of bullheads and catfish caught in the shallow waters of the Little and Big White Rivers. More than a few times he pulled ten to twenty-pound catfish from the murky waters of the Missouri. He was a survivor, and though he lost count of the lonely days and nights during his wanderings, rarely was he hungry or at the mercy of the elements.

Early lessons drawn from childhood memories served him well, especially memories of watching his father build hunting blinds or cozy brush shelters. Oliver built so many shelters along rivers and creeks—in shadowy draws or at the edges of cottonwood groves—that he used many of them more than once.

His favorite shelter stood near the confluence of the Little and Big White Rivers, at the head of a long draw just below a ridge. From a stone's throw away, it looked like nothing more than a pile of dry wood, but beneath it was a long, deep, intricately interwoven shelter with a front door, back door, and a smoke hole. Oliver had spent an entire winter there, not seeing another human being from December to March. Years later, those four solitary months were to stand him in good stead.

One late autumn Oliver wandered into a small town on the eastern edge of the reservation and walked into a store to buy coffee, failing to comprehend the sign above the door, which said "No Indians Allowed." However, four white ranch hands made certain Oliver understood the sign. With their coiled ropes, they beat him nearly senseless and then locked him in an icehouse. Fortunately for Oliver, the only window in the building was just large enough to squeeze through, which he did shortly after nightfall. By the next dawn he had managed to limp and crawl to a cold creek. After bathing his injuries, he walked upstream, staying in the icy current until sunset so he wouldn't leave scent for dogs to follow.

For the rest of his life, Oliver avoided that small town, couldn't drink coffee without feeling a twinge of pain somewhere, and religiously stayed away from groups of white men larger than two. And he never stopped looking for signs that said "No Indians Allowed."

On occasion Oliver stopped at the First Charger house to visit, never failing to bring food of some kind, most often two or three freshly killed rabbits. When he had money, which was not often, he would bring them flour, a slab of bacon, sugar, or coffee beans.

On one such visit Marie First Charger handed Oliver a letter addressed to him from the Bureau of Indian Affairs. To Oliver the letter was a dark omen, primarily because he knew he wouldn't be able to read it very well, but also because everyone knew nothing good ever came from the BIA agency. It was not until after the evening meal that he retreated to a secluded spot and opened the letter. Though he perused it over and over again, Oliver couldn't quite figure out what the letter said. In frustration he showed it to Marie First Charger, but her knowledge of English was not much better than Oliver's. In turn, she gave it to her oldest daughter, Phidell, who had graduated from the eighth grade and was able to decipher the letter for Oliver. As it turned out, it contained good news.

In one of their rare actions of genuine charity, the Bureau of Indian Affairs had been collecting lease money on Oliver's behalf for several years. The letter informed him that he had $580 in an account at the agency bank. Furthermore, the letter said, Oliver had inherited 320 acres of land from his parents and now was of age to take charge of it.

Oliver thought about what Phidell First Charger had translated as he rolled a cigarette. By the time he finished smoking it, he had come to a decision. If the letter was telling the truth, his wandering days were over and he would build himself a house.

With the letter in hand, he walked the twenty-seven miles from the First Charger Place to the agency—a two-day walk. In the agency town—a drab settlement with brick and wood frame houses—it took an entire day to figure out where to go with his letter. By the time he found the agency offices in a dimly lit brick building and was finally taken to the Realty Office, the agency had closed for the day. By noon of the next day Oliver had signed his name to several documents, none of which he understood. The realty officer had spent most of the morning just verifying Oliver's identity; then ironically, in spite of the seemingly complicated, officious process, the official had simply ended up taking Oliver's word, although of course he did not let Oliver know that.

By nightfall Oliver was halfway back to the First Charger place. Camping for the night, he sat staring at the envelope full of money in the orange glow of a campfire. It was all paper money, except for one silver dollar which Oliver liked because it had an eagle stamped on one side. The next day Marie First Charger told him to put the silver dollar away and keep it as a remembrance of his mother and father.

Soon afterward, Oliver went to see a man at a lumberyard in a small town some miles from his land on the riverbottom. There he bought a door, materials for roofing, four windows, three saws, two axes, a posthole digger, a drawknife, a hammer, a shovel, a pick, and a wheelbarrow to haul his purchases. He didn't know, of course, that the lumberman had charged him more than twice the value of the goods when he had seen Oliver's cash.

Oliver then bought a horse and a length of log chain. Since it was late spring he planted a garden and then prowled the cottonwood and oak groves along the river for logs. By the advent of summer, the four walls of the twelve-by-twenty-foot structure were ready for a roof. And by late summer, when the vegetable garden was well on its way, Oliver's house was finished.

In the meantime, in town word had gotten around about Oliver's house. The lumberyard owner had mentioned it to everyone he had come in contact with, raising an eyebrow as he wondered out loud where the young Indian might have gotten his money. No one could recall any robberies or burglaries in the area, and since cash in any amount was hard for anyone to come by in the late 1930s, it was not likely that any individual, white or Indian, would have had large sums of it around for anyone to steal. The lumberyard owner had forgotten, of course, that Oliver had pulled his cash out of an envelope clearly marked with the emblem of the Bureau of Indian Affairs.

Most people who knew the lumberyard owner were not surprised that he would openly question how Oliver might have gotten his money, although some asked the man why he had taken the money from Oliver if he had thought that it was ill-gotten booty of some sort. Such questions the lumberyard owner pretended not to hear.

One person who was interested in the growing rumors about Oliver Snow Bear was Della Wren, a newly hired county social worker who had just moved to the area. Being from Maryland she knew little about the communities in the county and was not at all disposed to learn anything about Indians. Her job was to look out for the less fortunate in the area, which in the 1930s included many whites as well as Indians. But she seemed especially intrigued with the case of Oliver Snow Bear.

Meanwhile, Oliver was tending to his garden and putting the finishing touches on his house. Anticipating a hard winter along the riverbottom, he had piled dry wood, which he would later haul to his place with the horse. Since he had bought a small stove for heating and cooking, he felt confident that the first winter in his new home would be comfortable, particularly since the vegetable garden was doing well and game was plentiful along the riverbottoms.

One day he was feeling especially good about things as he sat fashioning a plaque for his silver dollar. The plaque was nothing more than a leftover shake from his roof, in the center of which he carved out a perfect recessed circle into which he fit the silver dollar. Then he hung the plaque next to the window on the west wall just above his small wooden table, so he could glance at it as he looked out over the landscape. Every time he gazed at the silver dollar in the middle of the plaque, he wandered through the memories of his mother and father.

One gray afternoon Oliver was pulling weeds in his garden when he saw a car meandering across the prairie. Eventually it crossed a dry creek and wove through the soapweeds, stopping in front of Oliver's house. Oliver was surprised to see a little white woman step from the black car. A strange feeling went through him as she surveyed his place, holding a hand over her forehead to shade her eyes.

Like most Indians, Oliver was polite to whites. In fact, he was one of the most courteous young men anywhere. Courtesy was of utmost importance to the Lakota since to show courtesy was not to offend the dignity of others. Of course, many whites felt that such courtesy extended to them was deferential behavior, an acknowledgment of conquerors, so to speak.

As was his manner, Oliver approached the car, nodding politely, assuming that its single passenger was lost. However, the woman, who had been looking at a sheaf of papers in her hand, gave Oliver a cold, measuring stare with her shocking blue eyes. "Oliver Snow Bear?" she asked with a hollow, nasal whine.

Oliver nodded. But he was worried. A stranger knowing his name—especially a white woman—was not a good sign. He wondered if she worked at the BIA agency and had come to tell him that the money had been a mistake. He stopped a few yards from her, head bowed and hands clasped behind his back.

"Mr. Snow Bear," the woman continued as she boldly sized up the shy young Indian, "I am Della Wren, social worker for Redoubt County. I am here on official business."

Oliver understood some of what the woman said. Redoubt County was the northern county on the reservation, that much he knew. *Socialworker* and *officialbusiness* had no meaning for him, but he assumed, whatever they were they must be important to the woman—important enough to bring her out to the backcountry.

Della Wren consulted her sheaf of papers again. "You are an enrolled member of the tribe, Mr. Snow Bear?"

"Si-Sicangu Lakota," replied Oliver, hesitantly.

"Yes, that will do."

Eyes downcast, Oliver waited.

"Mr. Snow Bear, I need to look at your house."

A shiver of dread went through Oliver. It was about the money. Clearing his throat, he stepped hesitantly toward the house, stopped, and motioned for her to follow.

A bed, a small bench, a chair, a table, a wood-burning stove, a water bucket, and a washstand with a basin on it were the furnishings inside the small log house. Pegs to hang clothes were near the bed, and shelves for canned food and dishes were behind the stove, on which was a coffeepot. All in all, it was a neat, cozy little house.

However, Della Wren was appalled at the dirt floor. Then she immediately noticed the absence of books, a clock, or a calendar. Without waiting for an invitation, she pulled out the chair and seated herself at the table, on which she dropped her pile of papers as she rummaged in her purse for a pencil.

"Sit down, please," she said to Oliver, pointing toward the bench near the table.

Meekly, Oliver complied.

Glancing around the one-room house, Della Wren scribbled on a tablet.

"Mr. Snow Bear, how much land do you own?" she demanded.

Oliver cleared his throat. "Ah-ha-half section," he replied.

"Three hundred twenty acres? That much? My!"

"My folks," he tried to explain. "Their land."

"Yes, I thought as much, since you seem far too young to be an allottee."

She was referring to one of the consequences of the Dawes Act, or Homestead Act, of 1887, which had allotted land to individual Indians in the West—a process that had been started here by the BIA in the late 1890s and had been finished in 1910. Oliver's father, Seth Snow Bear, had been one of the original allottees to acquire 160 acres, as had Mary Yellow Eyes, Seth Snow Bear's mother. Oliver's mother had been an only child and the sole heir when her mother had died.

Della Wren, who looked a little displeased, then asked, "Do you lease your land?"

Oliver nodded. "Old Man Gallagher," he said. "Cows."

"Yes. You received a back payment, an accumulated sum of $580, did you not?"

Oliver thought he knew the gist of her question. The only thing he could think to do was reach in his back pocket and show her the folded envelope, which still contained over a third of the cash. He handed the envelope to the woman.

Della Wren quickly counted the money. "Almost $200," she mumbled to herself as she wrote on her tablet.

"Mr. Snow Bear, this is a lot of money. There must be a safer place to keep it than your back pocket. What if you should lose it somewhere? You would be destitute, I daresay."

Oliver nodded politely.

Reluctantly, it seemed to Oliver, she handed back the envelope. Oliver inwardly breathed a sigh of relief. She had given back the money. She was a government person, he decided, sent to check on what he had done with the lease money.

"House," he suddenly volunteered. "I put up house. Horse, I buy horse from Sam Nielsen to plow garden, haul wood." He pointed at the small, square cast-iron stove. "I buy, Seigelman's hardware."

Della Wren sighed. "Yes, you have indeed put your money to proper use ... it would seem." She paused as she openly studied his face. "Mr. Snow Bear, do you have relatives living?"

Oliver pondered the question. "Marie First Charger," he

finally replied. "I live with them—some years."

Della Wren flipped through the pile of papers, a frown on her pale face. "First Charger ... First Charger," she mumbled several times. "Are you certain they are related to you, Mr. Snow Bear?"

Oliver nodded. "I live with them. Before that, live with aunt, Effie Grass Lodge."

Della Wren shuffled her papers again, shaking her head. "Well," she decided, "I will need to go to the agency to verify that."

She began putting her papers back in order when she noticed the plaque on the wall with the silver dollar in it. Without hesitation she stood and took it down.

"Is this yours, Mr. Snow Bear?"

Oliver nodded, politely.

"Indeed! Where did you get it?"

Oliver hesitantly reached out and stood to touch the wooden plaque. "I make this," he explained. "Cut—carve with knife."

The woman touched the silver dollar, rubbing it lightly. "What about this, where did you get this?"

Oliver pulled out his money envelope once more. "Agency man give me."

"I see." Della Wren replaced the plaque and then pointing directly at the silver dollar, asked, "Tell me, Mr. Snow Bear, can you *make* one like this?"

Oliver frowned, remembering the few jobs he had had over the years and the money he had managed to earn. He began to nod.

"Yes," he told the woman. "I make."

"Indeed!"

Then to Oliver's relief Della Wren walked back to her car and drove away. He watched the car grow smaller and smaller as it meandered over the prairie, until it was nothing more than a black speck on the horizon.

That evening Marie First Charger and Phidell came for a visit, having walked nearly thirty miles. They brought dried meat, corn, flour, dishes—and a proposition. Phidell, now sixteen, was ready for marriage, and Oliver would need help to take care of his place. Phidell was a hard worker, not to mention a beautiful young woman. Since the age of fourteen she had had a serious interest in Oliver, an interest she had mentioned to her mother a year ago.

To prove her worth and her intentions, Phidell cooked an evening meal, complete with skillet bread, or sheepherder's bread, as some called it. The dried corn soup was the most delicious Oliver had ever tasted.

That evening Oliver gave his reply, and since the woman he had thought of as mother was now to be his mother-in-law, out of respect he did not look at her as he spoke. "You honor me," he said, looking at Phidell. "I will try hard to be a good husband and to provide for you."

Tears glistened in the girl's eyes as she looked toward her mother, who also surreptitiously wiped at her eyes. "I will walk with you through this life," Phidell replied. Soon Phidell and Marie First Charger returned home to make preparations for the wedding.

Days later Oliver walked to town to purchase new clothes, but he never bought the clothes, and it would be thirty years before he returned home.

Indians had been made citizens of the United States in 1924, reportedly as a reward for military service rendered by a few thousand Indians in World War I. The United States Congress enacted the legislation and granted citizenship without even asking Indians if they wanted to be American citizens. Oliver Snow Bear neither knew nor cared that he was an American citizen. He had been a free man all his life, surviving on his wits and his skills, owing nothing to any man, and servant to none. Understandably, he was confused when men he had never seen in his life surrounded him on the street, showed him a piece of paper which meant nothing to him, and took him away to a jail.

They had *jurisdiction*, they had told him, because he was a citizen. They could take him, they said, because he was a danger to *society*. Though he heard the words tossed at him as he was shoved into a car and driven to an imposing stone building, all he could understand was that his freedom was being taken from him.

After a cold night in a cramped jail cell, Oliver was led into a stark, sparse room and made to stand in front of a man seated behind a large table. Pale and stern, dressed in a dark suit, the man seemed to be more concerned with the pile of papers before him than he was with Oliver. Only once did he glance up, after calling out Oliver's name in a deep, gravelly voice.

Oliver nodded, relieved that at least someone knew who he was. Then the pale man spoke again, and a woman was ushered into the room—the woman who had come to Oliver's house asking questions. Della Wren was even less concerned about Oliver than the pale man was, not once glancing in his direction. She immediately found a chair—as she had in Oliver's house—and took a seat. This must be the way of white women, Oliver thought.

After a question from the pale man, the woman spoke for a very long time, fidgeting all the while, and sitting very straight on the edge of the large wooden chair. The pale man wrote things on a paper as the woman spoke. Neither the man nor the woman gave any sign that Oliver was in the room with them.

Oliver was left standing. Although he was stiff from a cold, sleepless night on a hard, wooden cot, he waited patiently, holding his hands clasped behind his back.

He could understand many of the white words the woman used, but some in between became obstacles, making it impossible to completely understand what the woman was talking about. Words like *house*, *garden*, and *alone* were not a problem. But words like *reclusive*, *incompetent*, and *simpleminded* were unknown to him. Oliver realized, however, that these strange activities concerned him directly since both the pale man and the woman occasionally pointed in his direction.

Finally, the pale man gave Oliver a long, thoughtful stare. Oliver thought he detected a glimmer of sadness or pity in the man's eyes, but it was gone in a heartbeat. Then the man turned toward a doorway and spoke loudly. Two men with silver badges pinned to their shirts came in and approached Oliver.

After another cold night in the tiny jail cell and a dawn meal of porridge, Oliver was escorted to a waiting car. The two men with silver badges drove him away. In the growing light of a cold, gray day, Oliver recognized much of the landscape at first, in the eastern part of the reservation where he had walked and camped many times. Then came roads, houses, and fences he didn't recognize—places and things of the white man. After they had crossed over the Missouri River, he saw small towns, machinery, and strange signs along the road. He was in a different land, a place he didn't know.

The men with badges were polite, stopping several times to see to his comfort, buy food, and let him stretch his legs. Once they opened the back compartment of the black car, and Oliver caught a glimpse of shackles and chains. Having seen such things on a prisoner once, he wondered if they were meant for him and was grateful the men had not used them.

When the sun went down and the land faded into the shadows of a strange half-light, they stopped along a narrow side road. It seemed to Oliver that there had been no evening, that day had evolved into night without a pause. He thought about Marie First Charger, Phidell, and his house, wondering how he would get word to them that something had happened to him.

Once he thought about running, knowing he could probably outrun the two men with badges. But he recalled the beating he had taken from the ranch hands with their coiled ropes. These two men had guns, and it was impossible to outrun guns. Besides, he didn't know the land they were in and could get lost. Instead, he put his hopes on the possibility that, wherever they were driving him, the men with badges would take him home afterwards. Oliver knew how to be patient and would wait to see how things turned out. Yet there was a loneliness seeping into his mind, a kind of loneliness he had never known. It made him shudder. Even the moon and stars seemed to turn away from him, although he knew they were behind the low clouds.

They had driven through a large town with more cars and buildings and streets than Oliver had ever imagined could exist anywhere. North, away from the town, the car turned onto a gravel road. A large sign stood where two high fences came together, announcing "State Mental Hospital." Behind the fences were broad, square-shouldered buildings with sharp edges.

The car's tires crunched on the gravel, as did Oliver's shoes when they stopped and he stepped out. His footsteps mingled with those of the men with badges, a hollow echo filling the night. Under a lighted landing, a thick oak door creaked open slowly and clicked shut behind them as the men with badges moved through, holding Oliver by the arms.

Oliver shuffled along reluctantly under more harsh lights. A strange, sharp odor he had never smelled assaulted his nose, seeming to ally itself with the stark wooden floors and bare white walls. Another door opened and snapped shut, and Oliver found himself in a small room without windows, where the smell was stronger. There the men with badges left him.

Oliver stared at the only object in the room, a long, dark bench with no back or sides. He was tired of sitting, but he sensed he was somehow vulnerable standing as he was in the middle of the room. Not certain if sitting was allowed, he retreated to a wall and cautiously leaned back on its cold surface.

Then the door opened. A man carrying a chair entered, followed by a woman in white with a strange, small glass object in her hand, an object she held carefully pointed upward.

The man put down the chair, sat, and stared at Oliver. After a moment, he spoke to the woman, who went back out through the door. Opening papers in his hands, the man looked carefully at them, with frequent glances up at Oliver.

"Oliver?" the man said, softly.

Oliver nodded tentatively.

"Oliver, do you know where you are?"

Oliver glanced around at the room. "In here," he replied.

"Yes, quite. You are in the State Mental Hospital. Have you heard of this place?"

Oliver shook his head no.

"When were you born, Oliver?"

With furrowed eyebrows Oliver considered the question. "In the spring," he replied.

"What month is it now?"

Oliver looked desperately at the opposite wall.

"Who is the president of the United States?"

The expression on Oliver's face did not change.

The man smiled. He was a young man with a gentle face, a face hovering on pity as he studied Oliver.

Uncomfortable with the stranger's scrutiny, Oliver stared at his feet. The door opened, and the woman in white entered again, accompanied by a man with bundles in his arms.

"Oliver," the young man called out. "Follow them." He pointed to the man and the woman. "It's late, they'll take you to your bed."

At the end of a long hallway with doors on either side, Oliver was led into a narrow room with four beds, all with gray mattresses rolled atop the springs. The woman unrolled a mattress, and the man quickly covered it with white sheets and bedcovers. Then he motioned for Oliver to follow him to the end of the room, where he pointed at the strangest contraption Oliver had ever seen—a large white bowl filled with water standing on the floor next to a second bowl atop four spindly legs. Although Oliver remembered seeing something like it at the Catholic boarding school, he hadn't used it then but had a feeling he would have no choice here. White people certainly lived in a strange world.

Then the door clicked shut, and Oliver was alone. Darkness

permeated the room completely as the bare bulb high overhead blinked out, filling him with a momentary panic. In another moment a second, much dimmer light came on, filling the room with a strange half-light.

Night passed with Oliver curled up on the edge of the bed atop the bedcovers. Now and then voices drifted through the walls, and once he heard a scream. Sleep escaped him until a gray light filled a long, narrow window just below the ceiling. He was in a fitful doze when the door opened and the young man who had spoken to him the night before entered with two other men.

Day passed with Oliver escorted from one room to another, facing divers groups of men, who regarded him with varying degrees of interest. That night he was taken to a different room, one occupied by five other men, all dressed in the same drab gray clothes that had been issued to Oliver.

Again he didn't sleep that night, only reclining on his bed listening to snores, coughs, and restless movements. The others, he knew, could sleep because they had been here for some time. Oliver wondered when he would sleep.

The following days blended monotonously into each other. Every morning Oliver trudged between his sleeping room and one filled with dark tables, high-backed wooden chairs, and people dressed in drab gray clothes. The people in gray clothes were difficult to adapt to. They were there in body, but some of them were not there in spirit. Facial expressions ranged from blank stares to confusion to amusement to anguish. To mask his own confusion, Oliver withdrew within himself.

One day he was let outside the building, into an open space with grass and trees. Though barefoot, he looked for a way to leave, but at every turn there was a high fence taller than he could reach. Beyond the fence were pastures, corn and wheat fields, and open country. To the west far past the horizon was home—his house and Phidell. When, he wondered, would he ever see home again?

A month passed, then two, then three. Autumn came, then winter, and then spring. During summer Oliver often stood at the fence looking west, toward home.

On the anniversary of his arrival, Oliver was questioned by three men.

"Do you know where you are?" one asked.

"Yes," replied Oliver. "I am here."

"What year is this, Oliver?"

"Nineteen thirty-eight," he told them. He had happened to look at a calendar that very morning. Though it had been no less confusing than white men's calendars had always been for him, he could read the year.

"When were you born?"

"In the spring."

"Where were you born?"

"Near the Big White River," he answered.

"Oliver, did you build a house?"

He nodded. "Yes."

"Did you have help? Did someone help you build it?"

Oliver shook his head. "I build it."

"Before you built your house, Oliver, where did you live?"

Oliver shrugged. "Everywhere."

"Where is 'everywhere,' Oliver?"

He shrugged again and struggled to find words they would understand. "I camp," he told them. "I make sleeping place, branches, leaves. I make fires, hunt, catch fish."

"In the winter and summer?"

He nodded, remembering the snug shelter of driftwood below a high ridge near the confluence of the Little and Big White Rivers.

The men exchanged glances, and one cleared his throat as he plucked a large coin from a vest pocket, sliding it across the table toward Oliver.

"Oliver," the man said, "what is this?"

"Dollar," he replied without hesitation. He had figured out

their purpose and the reason they had brought him here last spring. It was apparent that in the white man's world a person had to know a lot, and they thought he didn't know enough. That was the reason for all the questions.

"Oliver, can you make one of these?"

He nodded emphatically. "I make," he replied.

The men exchanged glances again and began putting away their papers.

The same questions were asked again at other times, but never again by a group of men. For a time Oliver wallowed in confusion and often sat alone in a corner of the large room full of chairs, tables, and people, wondering how he could learn more so he could leave this place. Try as he might he could find no answers, so he retreated into the only solace he had—his memories.

He wandered again through his travels, and each small adventure became a treasured memory; each meager meal of fish and chokecherries was a banquet, and each sunrise he had seen brought light to his drab existence. When he thought of these things, he became so immersed in them that the present ceased to exist. It was during these times that a man in a suit carefully observed him, though Oliver was unaware of him.

Days flowed into one another, seasons came and went, and years passed. One day Oliver noted that now and then a certain woman would bring newspapers and baskets of fruit to the people in the large room. At first, he took only an apple or a banana, then one day he picked up a newspaper and found that he could still read some of the white man's words.

The woman who brought the fruit and newspapers noticed and sat with Oliver. Once she pointed to a word and pronounced it, and Oliver realized that here was the answer.

After that, he grabbed every newspaper the woman brought in. After pointing to words he didn't know, she would pronounce them. Soon he looked forward to her visits and after some weeks began to see the world outside through the words in the newspapers. Oliver kept as many of the papers as he could, those that held no interest for anyone else. Carefully folding them, he piled them beneath his bed, keeping them neat and dusting them regularly.

One day the woman who brought newspapers came with the terrible news that her husband had been killed at a place called Pearl Harbor. After that, she came only one last time, to say good-bye and bring Oliver a book entitled *Last of the Mohicans*. Only Oliver was sad to see her go, only Oliver shared her pain. He never saw her again, though some weeks later she wrote him a long letter encouraging him to continue reading.

Since no one else ever brought newspapers to the large room or gave Oliver a book to read he did the only thing he could think of. He read every newspaper over and over again, and read the book several times.

One day he asked a new man in a suit for a newspaper and learned about a place called Korea. He saw the year at the top of the newspaper's front page, and, counting backwards, determined that he had been inside the fence thirteen years.

The places beyond the fence were changing. Buildings were creeping closer to it. Airplanes frequently flew overhead, and he noticed a different roaring sound that some had. The highway running north and south had been widened, and more cars and trucks traveled it each day. There were also more lights in the distance at night, and the tall poles along the highway were strung with more lines.

Inside, the people in gray clothes came and went, although several who had been there when Oliver arrived were still inside. The men in suits and women in white also came and went—with greater frequency than the people in gray.

Every year someone sat Oliver at a large table, opened a pile of papers, and asked him questions. And every year he answered them, hoping that what he had learned from his book and newspapers would help him to be able to leave and go home. But each year he was disappointed.

Then once one of the women in white showed him a new room with nothing but books and magazines, and Oliver began burying himself in them whenever he could, reading and studying pictures. The world was such a large place, and his life was limited to such a small part of it, he mused. But the books and magazines did what he couldn't do for himself: they took him beyond the fence and the cold brick walls and away from the gray people.

One day he sat down and wrote a letter, a letter of apology to Phidell First Charger:

> *They took me away to this place because I do not know enough to live in their world. I could not marry you because I am in this place. Life is hard, but you are a good woman. I feel now you have turned into a wife for someone. That is alright. Please forgive me for the trouble I have given you.*

The woman who was in charge of the room full of books, which he learned was called the library, helped him address and mail the letter. It was the first time he had reached out to the world he had left behind.

The world inside the fence, inside the cold bricks, was changing, too. Inside, everyone who worked there still was white-skinned, but their clothes had changed. Women were wearing men's trousers, and their hair was shorter, while men's hair was longer. The men in suits, whom Oliver now knew were called doctors, didn't always wear suits, and some of them were now women.

Moving pictures on a wall and inside a small box had been strange and frightful things for Oliver at first. But like books they had become a link to the world outside. One day, however, like many people in the outside world, he watched in confusion as the president of the United States—a man named John Kennedy—was killed by a man with a rifle. Days later the television room was filled with people watching as a flag-draped coffin was carried behind a prancing black horse.

In the hush of the moment, Oliver hardly noticed that someone had put a piece of paper in his hand. After the television was
shut off, he looked at the paper, which was a letter from Phidell
First Charger telling about her life since they had been abruptly
separated:

> *Father John Steinmark is helping me to write this.*
> *There is a lot to tell. My mother died seven years ago.*
> *My younger sisters are all married. I have been living*
> *with Ethel to help care for her children. She has not*
> *been well. We heard what happened to you. Mom*
> *cried for months. There is nothing to forgive. I said I*
> *would marry you, so I will wait. Write again.*

For the first time in twenty-five years, Oliver wept. He walked
outside into the cold November air—for now he had the freedom to walk the grounds—and stood at the west fence, looking
off toward the horizon, toward home, which until now had
existed only in memory. While he wept, his yearning to go home
resurged anew.

He wrote to Phidell, and in a few weeks her reply came. Her
letter was long, filling in details about the intervening years. The
house he had built was still there but falling apart. Old Man
Gallagher was still alive and leasing Oliver's land through the
Bureau of Indian Affairs.

After the initial exchange of letters, the information Phidell
provided ceased to be important. She became his image of
home, and that was all he cared about. Soon their letters flowed
steadily back and forth, week after week, month after month,
and—sadly—year after year.

Then one day in 1966 home became more than a dream
when a young doctor, Dr. Morehead, arrived to work at the State
Mental Hospital. Whatever the reason, he took special interest in
Oliver's situation, visiting with Oliver at every opportunity.

One morning a young Indian man was in Dr. Morehead's
office as Oliver walked in, a Lakota who spoke Oliver's first language fluently. "Oliver," said Dr. Morehead, "this is Richard Last.

He's from your reservation and knows some of your relatives. I've asked him to come here to help me get to the bottom of some things. Is that okay with you?"

Oliver nodded, sensing a different mood in the room. He couldn't put his finger on it, but he liked what he was feeling.

Dr. Morehead opened a drawer and took out a silver dollar, watching Oliver closely as he put the coin on the desk. "I have two questions, Oliver," he said. "First, about this coin. Then, about a word."

Oliver leaned back, took a deep breath, and waited.

"Tell me about this coin, Oliver."

"It—it's a silver dollar."

"Why is it important to you?"

"I kept it to remember my mother and father by."

"I see. Is there anything else about this that you can tell me?"

Oliver shook his head. "No."

"Do you remember a woman by the name of Mrs. Della Wren?"

Oliver nodded.

Dr. Morehead, his youthful face intense, consulted a file of papers and then looked up again. "Mrs. Wren was a social worker for Redoubt County. She was the person, Oliver, who sent you here thirty years ago."

Oliver nodded again. He had figured as much. There was only one thing he didn't know. "Why?"

Dr. Morehead glanced at Richard Last briefly. "Because of this." He touched the silver dollar. "Or at least I think so."

"She asked me once about my silver dollar—the one I kept to remember my mother and father."

"Yes, I know. I want to ask you the same question, and that's where Mr. Last comes in."

The doctor picked up the coin and carefully consulted his notes. "Oliver," he said gently, "can you make one of these?"

"Yes," Oliver answered.

"Now, Oliver, tell me *in Lakota* how to say 'I make money.'"

Oliver sighed and thought. It had been such a long time since he had spoken to anyone in Lakota. *"Ma-mazaska wakage,"* he said.

Dr. Morehead turned to Richard Last. "Tell me, Richard, is there another way to say that in Lakota?"

"Yes, there is," the man replied without hesitation. "One can also say *mazaska wakamna*, which means 'I earn money.'"

The doctor smiled sadly and shook his head. "You mean the Lakota words in this instance for *make* and *earn* are interchangeable?"

"Yes," Last replied. "Make can mean earn, earn can mean make."

"It is possible, then, that someone using the word for *make* does not mean it literally."

"That's correct," affirmed the young Indian.

"So when Oliver answered Mrs. Wren's question thirty years ago—as he just answered mine—he could not have meant that he could craft, or produce, a silver dollar?"

"No. He meant that he could work to earn one," Richard confirmed.

Dr. Morehead closed the file of papers, stood, and walked to Oliver. "My friend," he said, "in about a week, ten days at the most, it will be my pleasure to take you home. I hope that someday you will find it in your heart to forgive the world, to forgive us, for our arrogance and narrow-mindedness. And, by the way, when I tried to locate Mrs. Wren, I learned that she went insane one day and ran screaming down the streets of Cold River without a stitch of clothing on. As a matter of fact, she has been in Ordway Six, two buildings over, for the last ten years. That's the wing where we keep the crazy ones."

She was waiting in front of the post office in Cold River where he had asked her to in his letter. Tears ran down her face as she clasped his hands. He recognized her but could see that thirty years had taken their toll. But although she was thin, she was not frail, and there was the same sparkle in her eyes that he had seen at the time of their betrothal.

"I am honored you have joined your path to mine," he said to Phidell, in Lakota.

"There has been no other," she replied.

A man emerged from a car nearby and approached, making himself known to Dr. Morehead and regarding Oliver with great interest. After a moment, the two approached the reunited couple.

"Oliver," said Dr. Morehead, "this is Mr. Draper from the Bureau of Indian Affairs. He and I have been in touch, regarding your land."

The paunchy man in a rumpled suit extracted an envelope from a leather case and held it out to Oliver. "Sir," he said, "this is money paid into your account at the Indian Bank at the agency. This is a U.S. government check for the amount of $13,500. It's your lease money paid in by the Gallagher family. I've talked to the banker here, who will be more than happy to open an account for you."

Oliver's hand shook as he took the money and turned to thank Dr. Morehead.

"Oh, that's not all," the doctor said, taking an envelope from an inside coat pocket. "This is from the state—the $200 that was confiscated by Mrs. Wren. At 20 percent interest compounded annually, this check amounts to $3,125. It doesn't replace thirty years of lost time, but it can help to make the rest of your life easier. Take care of yourself, my friend."

Since it was still early in autumn, Oliver and Phidell repaired their house and moved into it—thirty years later than planned. Father John Steinmark married them in July and became their good friend. Now and then, when he preached sermons on faithfulness and patience, he invoked the names of Phidell First Charger Snow Bear and Oliver Snow Bear as epitomizing those virtues.

Phidell and Oliver lived as man and wife for fourteen years, though they couldn't have children. In the spring, summer, and autumn, Oliver hardly set foot in his own house, preferring the sun, wind, and rain on his face. And often in winter he would remain outdoors for a long time as well.

One day, her curiosity overflowing, Phidell asked her husband how he felt about the social worker, Mrs. Wren.

He answered without hesitation. "I pity her," he said. "I knew many like her there, where I was—the people with gray clothes."

On a crisp autumn day in 1981 as he sat outside his house waiting for coffee to boil over the firepit, Oliver Snow Bear fell dead. He died happy.

Phidell buried him on a rise near their house, remembering what he had said about his selection of a location for the house: "From here I can see who is coming."

During the ten more years Phidell lived, her house was often filled with nieces and nephews, for she was grandmother to their children. But despite the days filled with activity every night until she died, before she turned out the light, she would touch the silver dollar in the plaque on the wall near the window.

Cozy by the Fire

▲   Jeremy Blue stopped his truck at the fork above Black
▲   Pipe Creek and contemplated the blowing snow. Black
▲   Pipe School was four miles to the right, to the southwest.
▲   Home was forty miles to the left, to the south. He want-
▲   ed badly to be home.

As attendance counselor, or really the truant officer, of Black Pipe School, at one time or another he had traveled every back road in the northwestern part of the reservation. It was Friday just past 2:00 in the afternoon. The student he had checked on had been home with a bad cold. That information could keep until Monday, especially since he didn't like the way the wind was whipping the snow around. His compact truck was too small and light to fight the snowdrifts that could block a road so easily here on the open prairies. Winter was no time to gamble with weather. Jeremy shifted into first and turned south, toward home. It was doubtful the principal would fire him for being sensible about winter weather, he felt.

Since most of the local residents were Indians, the county highway maintenance officials were of the opinion that the Bureau of Indian Affairs should maintain the roads in this area, despite the fact that the road had been appropriated by the right of eminent domain by the county years ago. As a result of constant tit-for-tat legal brinkmanship, the roads in the Black Pipe District were not paved and always the last to be plowed after heavy snows.

Soon low clouds scudded from the west so suddenly Jeremy didn't see them coming, and fresh flakes mingled with the snow being already whipped about. Depressing the accelerator, he heard the little four-cylinder motor groan just to gain a little speed. A January blizzard was nothing to fool with, not here on the prairies. Every winter, it seemed, someone froze to death, and Jeremy didn't want to be this year's statistic.

But unless the weather became decidedly worse in the next hour, he'd be home before Celine. She would be surprised if he picked up their four-year-old daughter, Cora, from Head Start. And maybe he'd even cook supper. That would really amaze his wife, since it had been about two months since he'd burned that pot of stew.

Suddenly, a wall of snow charged Jeremy from the northwest. He watched it advance, unable to alter the situation. One moment he could see the gravel road and the three-strand barbed-wire fences on either side, while in the next the world was a shroud of blue-white.

Jeremy did the only thing possible—he stopped the truck. Although the fence to the right was just twenty feet away, at the moment nothing existed but himself, his truck, and the blue-tinted whiteness. Flakes rattled against the truck, and the wind howled, a low, mournful cry that made him shudder. He turned up the heat in the cab.

By 4:15 Jeremy had turned the engine on and off four times. He knew it was better to conserve fuel, to assume that the blizzard would last for hours, if not days. Fortunately, he had filled the gas tank this morning.

As the wind howled and he felt like the last person left on earth, Jeremy took stock of his situation. He was dressed appropriately in a down-filled coat and heavily lined gloves. A cap and

wool scarf were on the seat next to him, but there was one pre-
caution he had overlooked. A week ago he had removed the
wool blanket usually kept behind the seat for just such an even-
tuality because Celine had wanted to wash it.

He also had no food or water. Looking in the glove compartment, he found a small cup. He could pack it with clean
snow and let it melt in the cab. The water problem was solved.
Next to heat, water was the most critical thing. A momentary
bravado seized him—he was certain of survival.

Jeremy ran a hand through his thick black hair, then rubbed
his long, narrow face. He was on the edge of handsome with a
friendly twinkle always in his light brown eyes. His long, narrow
nose and wide mouth were typical Lakota features. Jeremy was
one-quarter shy of being full blood. His mother was Sicangu and
his father Mniconju, with the French blood on his mother's side.

He'd left the reservation for a while, but had had an awful
experience in Minneapolis. The Job Corps school in Ronan,
Montana, had been better. There he'd learned finish carpentry,
but more importantly, he'd met Celine. Home was on the reservation. Here he felt a connection he couldn't define—a strong
sense of identity and belonging, even in the middle of a blizzard.

Light faded about 5:20, making Jeremy feel more alone.
When he attempted to start the engine again, the truck balked
and missed badly when it did, with one cylinder obviously not
firing. He let it run for fifteen minutes, then shut it down. After
the cab began to lose its warmth, he braved the wind and stinging snow and went out to look under the hood.

The headlights reflecting off him revealed an engine compartment filled with white. Snow had blown in over the sides of
the engine, between the fan and radiator. Jeremy scooped out
handfuls of snow, especially from around the spark plug wires,
the belts which turned the fan, and the back of the radiator. The
wind was merciless, tugging at the hood and piercing him with
a chill as he worked. Finally he slammed the hood down and got

back into the quiet cab. Hesitantly, he turned the ignition key, relieved when the engine turned over more easily, though one cylinder still missed occasionally.

So thick was the snow that it reflected the headlights' glare back at him. Shutting off the lights reduced his world to the cab's interior. He turned on the dash lights, telling himself he needed to keep an eye on the gauges but knowing he wanted the dim but reassuring glow.

Reluctantly, Jeremy considered the facts of his situation. First the positive aspects: he had plenty of gasoline, and the truck was starting, though he would have to keep the engine compartment free of snow. Next the negative aspects: the closest community was Black Pipe, nearly eight miles straight west, while the nearest ranch was ten miles to the south. The blizzard showed no sign of abating, snow was piling up around his truck and seeping in the passenger-side door, and he had no idea how long the storm would last.

He shut down the motor and turned off the dash lights to conserve battery power. Near total darkness consumed him as the wind rocked his truck slightly. Cold began to creep in almost immediately. He wound his watch to make sure it would keep going, for some reason not wanting to lose track of time.

Celine would be home by now. She would be safe since their sedan was newer and heavier than the truck, the Head Start Center was only half a mile from their house, and she was a good driver. But she would start worrying since he should have been home by now.

Jeremy was glad he had recently stocked up on supplies. Yesterday, he'd checked their propane tank, which was more than 50 percent full, plenty for heating and cooking. They'd just shopped for groceries so there was lots of food in the house. Celine and Cora would be fine.

"Thank God," he muttered, surprising himself since he was not a religious man. Easter and Christmas and funerals were the only times he'd go to church, and then only to please Celine. He couldn't remember the last time he had really prayed, wondering if he ever had, although he did believe in God. Some called him *Wakantanka*, the Great Spirit.

Jeremy's cousin, Cornilius Blue, scoffed at Christianity, at the arrogance of any religion which portrayed itself as the only religion or the one true religion. Cornilius was a traditionalist and, unlike Jeremy, a fluent Lakota speaker. Cornilius believed in *Wakantanka* but never preached or proselytized, never tried to convert anyone to his way of believing. "Religion isn't about converting anyone, it isn't a contest for souls," he would say. "It's about living principles and beliefs, every day."

Jeremy knew that Cornilius participated in many of the traditional ceremonies, like the ones for purification and healing. There was a standing invitation for Jeremy to also participate, an invitation extended only once years ago but still valid.

Jeremy looked around at the darkness which held him in its cold embrace, listening to the mournful howl of the wind. He yearned for the light of dawn, knowing it was nearly fourteen hours away. Was God, *Wakantanka*, in the darkness, he wondered, or was he only a god of light? If he ever got home, he would ask Cornilius and maybe even attend some traditional ceremonies to learn more about what others in the tribe believed. Would Cornilius feel less alone at a time like this because of his beliefs?

At 6:30 he started the engine. It sputtered, and the missing was noticeable. However, warmth returning to the cab was a welcome change in the monotony of darkness and cold. Before he started the engine the next time, he would need to clear out snow, he surmised.

An hour and a half dragged by after he shut down the engine. He positioned his legs diagonally toward the passenger side and flexed his calf and thigh muscles. Then he leaned an arm on the back of the seat and rested his head on it, dozing a little but always aware of the rocking motion of the truck and the persistent howl of the wind.

When the cold bordered on being uncomfortable, he forced himself outside to check under the hood. As anticipated, it was packed full of snow, and he scooped it out until his gloves were soaked and his back ached from bending over. Back in the cab, his heart sank when the engine failed to start after the first few turns of the key. Not wanting to run down the battery, he reopened the hood, unhooked each spark plug wire, wiped each plug terminal as dry as he could with the end of his shirt sleeve, and blew on the end of each spark plug wire.

Then with a mixture of dread and hope he turned over the starter again, and was weak with relief when the engine caught. He let it run for half an hour, although it never really idled smoothly. Moisture was probably getting into the carburetor, he feared. He laid his wet gloves directly under the heater vent and turned the fan on high. The heavy odor of wet leather filled the cab. Prompted by a sudden whim, he decided to check the carburetor while the motor was still running.

His fears were justified. Ice was forming around the intake throat. Gingerly, with trembling fingers, he lifted out as much of the paper-thin ice as he could, knowing that any amount of moisture sucked into the carburetor jets would stall the engine. Then it wouldn't matter how much fuel was in the tank. The engine simply wouldn't run.

Once back in the cab, he couldn't stop shivering, although it was hot inside. The storm had not abated, and gave no indication that it would. If anything, the wind was blowing harder. There was no choice but to conserve fuel, and to do that he would have to turn off the engine.

Turning off the engine would mean two possibilities, neither a certainty. The engine would start again, or it would not. And if it started the next time, what about the time after that?

Images of Celine and Cora filled his mind. They were warm and safe, he knew that. But to see them again he needed to do what he had to to keep himself safe. To see them again, he would have to turn off the truck's engine to conserve fuel. Fingers trembling, he reached for the key. It was such a slight movement to turn it to the left, requiring hardly any effort, but nonetheless bearing the burden of life or death.

The sudden absence of engine and heater fan noise was all too quickly filled with the sound of the wind. Jeremy looked into the darkness. "God," he said, "if you're out there, don't forget where I am." And then added, "Take care of my family."

Time passed. Then cold nibbled at him, teasing him to wakefulness. It took a moment or two to realize he'd been sleeping, with his head leaning against the cold glass of the back window and his hands tucked under his armpits. Peering closely at the luminous dial of his watch, he saw that it was just after 9:00 P.M. It was freezing in the cab, yet he noticed that the wind had died down some, with occasional lulls.

Heartened, he shifted around to start the engine. But the sound of a stiff, balky engine filled him with a piercing, frigid fear that settled between his shoulder blades like an ice ball shoved against his skin. He pumped the accelerator once and turned the key again but got the same result—a reluctant groan.

Reasoning that the battery still held a good charge, he jumped out and opened the hood. In two or three minutes, he cleared snow out again, blew on the spark plug wires, dried off the plug terminals, and then lifted off the air filter housing to look at the carburetor. It was loaded with ice, frozen from the condensation as the carburetor had sucked in cold air. He removed as much of the ice as he could, knowing that it was an exercise in futility, a gesture of hope rather than a mechanical remedy.

Still the engine stubbornly refused to start. Back under the hood, he shoved his handkerchief down into the throat of the carburetor, hoping to soak up as much moisture as possible. Yet he knew that it was a hopeless effort, if moisture had reached the intake valves of the cylinders. After climbing back in the cab, he sighed in despair as the engine groaned and groaned without starting.

The reason for his next actions he would never understand. He jumped out, opened the hood, detached the cables, and carried the battery into the cab, placing it on the floor of the passenger side. Perhaps it was nothing more than an act of defiance, a refusal to yield to the storm. Not that it would matter in the end.

Jeremy's only concern now was to stay warm somehow. And the only way he could think of doing this was to get out of the cab every hour and run in place beside the truck. Just after 10:00 P.M. he started this routine, noticing with slight hope that the wind was definitely abating.

While he was outside the truck, something caught his eye during a brief lull—a small, dim spot of light to the east. Staring at it in disbelief, he tried to remember who might live in the area. Since school had started he had been back and forth on this road at least eighty times, and he couldn't recall having seen a building this close to the highway anywhere near this location. And there was no turnoff or gate to indicate that anyone lived here. Of course, a gate could be anywhere.

Nevertheless, a light was there, dim but steady, disappearing when the wind gusted and blew snow, and appearing again during each lull.

Cold drove Jeremy back into the cab. He scraped the frost off the inside of the window and looked through the hand-sized space, still seeing the dim light.

After twenty minutes of sitting in one position and staring at the light, his neck began to get stiff. In all that time the orange pinpoint in the darkness had burned steadily. The wind was losing its intensity. One lull was just over five minutes in duration.

A compelling thought occurred to Jeremy. Since the wind was dying down, he could see the light more clearly with each passing minute. If he wanted to attempt reaching the light, now would be the time, before the wind picked up again.

The thought made Jeremy shudder with apprehension and indecision. The cardinal rule when caught in a blizzard on an open road was to stay with your vehicle. Every single winter casualty in the past had occurred when people tried to walk for help and had died of exposure because they had lost their way.

Still, the light was close—or it appeared to be close. When the wind picked up again—and Jeremy knew it would—the blowing snow would hide the light. Furthermore, the truck wouldn't start, and the temperature was dropping with each passing hour.

With the wind abating significantly, Jeremy reasoned, he could walk toward the light, and if it was too far away or he lost sight of it he could follow his tracks back to the truck. There was logic there, he told himself. But was it logic based on sound judgment—or born of desperation?

In an instant Jeremy reached a decision. He found himself standing in the relatively snow-free pocket next to the truck. Beyond that was knee-deep snow, he guessed, although he really didn't know because it was so dark. His guess was based on experience with countless ferocious winter storms.

When Jeremy began to walk, his calculations were confirmed—the snow was knee deep, and walking in it was difficult. Stepping over the barbed-wire fence, he looked back toward his truck, which now appeared as an elongated, dark shadow amidst the lighter shadows of the snowfield.

To the east the light seemed brighter, a persistent glow, a beckoning hope. He paused momentarily, wondering if he was hallucinating, but concluded that the only unknown was the light. Every other miserable thing—the snow, the piercing cold, the stalled truck—was real enough. There was only one way to prove if the light was real or an hallucination.

Struggling through the deep snow warmed him, though after a few yards he was panting. To his relief, the light was still there, defying cold and darkness.

Before he was too far into the snowy pasture, he paused to look at his tracks. They were deep, and only a steady blow would fill them quickly—a good sign, he decided, and pushed on.

Progress was slow but steady, and after a time the light seemed to take a different shape. No longer was it a simple pinpoint of light but seemed to be rectangular. He was encouraged when after a few more heart-pounding steps, the rectangle of light seemed larger.

Jeremy rested and stared at the light, hands on hips, panting. Distances on the open prairies were often deceiving under the best of circumstances, but he guessed the light was only a hundred yards or so away. Behind him his truck had disappeared into the cold, dark gloom. Ahead of him, still out of reach, was the dim, beckoning light. For a few seconds he had to suppress panic, suddenly understanding the phrase "no man's land." Nevertheless, he continued doggedly toward the light, hoping for a warm respite from the cold and perhaps a telephone. A call to Celine would ease her mind.

For several yards he felt himself on a slight downward incline, and after sinking nearly hip deep in snow guessed he was in an old creek bed. Luckily, the dry creek bed was only ten yards across—but ten of the coldest, cruelest yards he'd ever walked in his life. His heart pounding wildly, his breath coming in sharp gasps, he finally reached the opposite bank. From there it was a fight to climb up the bank without secure footholds. Finally, after being face down on a narrow ledge, he managed to pull himself gradually upright. With diminished strength, he stood staring with renewed hope at the orange glow in a window.

Pulling off his cold, stiff gloves he wiped his eyes, still afraid it might be an hallucination, but now the window had definite characteristics. It was a narrow rectangle with four long panes— two in the bottom half, two in the top. Somewhere behind and to the right of the glass was the source of light, although it was dim.

Hope rekindled, his judgment vindicated, Jeremy nearly ran the last forty yards toward the light, unmindful that his trousers and shoes were soaked and beginning to freeze solid.

Suddenly, a low, dark shape emerged from the darkness. A

house! The lighted window was near the east corner of the northern end of the building. Instinctively, he headed for the east side, sensing that the door was there. On the east side were two more windows of the same size and shape, equal distances from the door in the middle. In the relative calm of the lee side, he could hear his own panting and his thudding heartbeats. Pausing to calm himself, he peered into the closest window but could see nothing through the thin layer of frost on the inside. Then he went to the door and lifted a hand to knock.

After the door swung open, a face appeared in the opening, mostly in shadows, though he could see long, gray braids falling over a barely visible pattern on a calico dress and a pair of old, gentle eyes calmly assessing him. Welcome warmth wafted out from the fire inside, along with another mysterious, more encompassing kind of warmth.

He pointed his arm. "My truck is stalled," he explained immediately. "Out on the road. It won't start. I saw the light in your window."

The door opened wider, and a small hand gnarled with age motioned him to step inside. After a few seconds his eyes began adjusting to the dim light, and he realized that the sources of light were three old-fashioned kerosene lamps, one on either side of the room and one above a stone fireplace against the west wall. Then he noticed that the house, which was made of logs and chinked with mud, was only one long, north-south room.

Turning toward a dull, metallic clanking sound, he saw an old man turn from a pot-bellied stove after closing its door. The man spoke something unintelligible but pointed toward a wooden bench close to the stove.

Jeremy unzipped his down coat as he crossed the room. The woman watched him without looking directly at his face. Her calico dress was blue, he could see now, and it hung down to her ankles. She was slight, almost frail, yet she moved with a graceful dignity he often saw in old Lakota women. Her face was gentle, seamed with creases, and a slight smile turning up the edges of her mouth.

The man wore a light-colored shirt and baggy trousers held up with dark suspenders. His gray hair was thin and loose, hanging nearly to his collar, while his face was even more deeply creased than the woman's, with pronounced cheekbones, a strong, straight nose, and a wide mouth. His eyes were dark and inquisitive.

"My name is Jeremy Blue," he went on. "I'm from Antelope Hills. I work over here at the Black Pipe School, and I was on my way home when the storm caught me."

They nodded affably.

As he shed his coat and began unlacing his boots, Jeremy took a quick, unobtrusive survey of the room. On the south end was a large, old-fashioned, cast-iron stove with overhead warming bins and a side hot water reservoir. It had been years since he'd seen one like it.

Under the southernmost window on the east side, was a rough-hewn wooden table with three high-backed chairs. To the left of the stove, were several shelves on which were various cans and jars. In the southwest corner, was a wooden barrel three feet high next to a stand with a white washbasin. From a peg on the wall above the barrel hung a tin dipper, for water. The floor was made of wide wooden planks, and the pot-bellied stove was in the middle of the room.

On the north end was a low bed, obviously homemade. Under the patchwork quilt of various dark colors was an uneven mattress of some sort, and next to the head of the bed was a very tall dresser.

Jeremy laid his wet gloves and boots close to the stove and stretched out his legs to dry his wet trousers. "I didn't think anyone lived around here, so I was very glad to see your light," he said, conversationally.

They nodded once again.

He looked out the north window and saw snow fly by in the openings the frost hadn't covered. The wind was picking up, but he couldn't hear it. Except for the crackle of the wood burning in the stone fireplace and soft clunks as the old woman performed some chore at the table, there was a deep silence.

Then in a firm but polite tone, the man spoke, but Jeremy couldn't understand, although he realized he was hearing Lakota; even though Jeremy knew many Lakota words and phrases, he couldn't speak the language with much confidence.

The couple was looking at Jeremy, motioning toward the table, which had been set. They were offering him a meal. He crossed the room and sat down at the table. On it were a large, dark blue enameled plate with white speckles, a large cup, and several utensils. On the plate was some delicious-smelling stew and a piece of skillet bread. The cup was filled nearly to the brim with hot, strong coffee. Overjoyed to have found shelter from the storm, food was an added blessing he hadn't expected, but then he knew that any guest in a Lakota home was always invited to eat. It would be extremely rude not to accept the invitation.

"Thanks," he said, sitting down, then translated it to Lakota—"*Pila mayapelo.*" They nodded, smiling, and moved away to do various chores as he ate.

Jeremy had never tasted such good stew and guessed that the meat was deer. His grandmother had often made skillet bread, a version of sheepherder's bread. She would simply add flour to water until she could knead the dough out flat, and then fry it in a hot skillet with only a little grease. Dipped in soup, or stew as he did now, it was wonderful. The hot, strong coffee had obviously been made in the old way, in which grounds were dropped into the top of a pot and then boiled.

A warm house and good food revived him. He stammered his thanks again in Lakota.

"Grandmother, here are your dishes."

It was customary among his grandparents' generation to call attention to empty plates and cups after a meal, to show that the gift of a meal had been accepted with a good heart. An empty plate meant that the food was good.

Smiling, the old woman promptly approached with a small black kettle and ladled another generous helping of stew onto his plate and then gave him another piece of skillet bread. The old man poured more coffee. Jeremy smiled his appreciation and eagerly dug into the stew. This was the other kind of warmth he had felt when the door had first been opened.

Finally finished, he gently pushed the plate toward the center of the table and carried his coffee cup to the bench near the stove.

The old woman ventured a question. He knew she wanted to know if he had eaten enough.

He nodded. "Yes," he assured her. "It was very good."

As yet the couple had not said who they were, and he didn't want to be rude by asking. He had not seen them before anywhere. But they were here, and if it weren't for them he could still be in the truck in real danger of freezing to death. Fed, warm, and safe, there was no reason to question his benefactors about anything.

Snow was flying by the partially frosted window. The wind was picking up, but he still couldn't hear it.

Jeremy stared at the cup as he held it between his hands, savoring the heat it provided, as well as the warm memories. There was a time in his childhood when his grandparents had cooked coffee by boiling it loose in big pots and then serving it in dark blue enameled cups speckled with white. Percolators were the thing now, along with preground coffee and china cups with handles a man couldn't get a finger through.

A rustle nearby pulled him from his memories. The old woman had unrolled some kind of a mattress a few feet from the stove and covered it with a dark blue wool blanket and a thick, patchwork quilt. Glancing at him only briefly, she pointed to the bed and spoke softly but firmly. Though it was difficult to comprehend Lakota words, he knew she was telling him that it was time to turn in. He could see they were now preparing for bed as well, almost as if they had been waiting for him to come to their house before they went to bed.

Jeremy nodded and removed his damp socks to lay them alongside his gloves and shoes. The old man had extinguished two kerosene lamps and carried the third to the high dresser next to their wood frame bed.

Jeremy's bed was a feather tick, which didn't surprise him since these old people were obviously not fond of modern conveniences, or chose to live without them. Waiting until the third lamp had been extinguished, he took off his trousers and spread them out close to the stove, hoping they would dry overnight. The patchwork quilt was heavy and the blue blanket a little scratchy, but the vinyl seat covers in the truck could never have provided such comfort. He thought of Celine and Cora, wishing there was some way he could let them know he was safe.

Fatigue and relief rolled over Jeremy as he pulled the quilt around his shoulders. Before he fell asleep, he had a thought. *Thank you* he said into the darkness. *Thank you for keeping me safe.*

A faint metallic clank awoke him. Rubbing his eyes, he felt a slight chill in the air. The old man was at the stove stoking the burned down coals back to life. Jeremy soon heard wood crackle as it caught fire, and the old man closed the stove door.

Then the strong odor of fresh coffee reached him. A soft voice spoke as he turned. The old woman had put a steaming cup of coffee on the bench. Pushing the heavy quilt aside, he reached for the cup, only then remembering that his trousers were near the pot-bellied stove. But the old couple discreetly kept their backs turned, busying themselves with chores as he reached for his pants and put them on.

The old man called his attention to the washbasin in the corner as he poured in hot water. The old woman laid a worn-out towel on the stand. Sipping his coffee as he crossed the cold floor on bare feet, he bent over the basin and washed his face. Already waiting for him at the table was a plate with two pieces of hot skillet bread fresh off the cooking stove and a generous helping of honey.

Bright light poured in through the windows, and Jeremy could tell that it was a cold, cloudless day. When he peered out the window above the table, he was happy to see that the wind had blown most of the snow away. Apparently during the night it had stopped snowing, but the wind had kept blowing—one of winter's quirks here on the northern prairies. If the wind had blown hard enough, the road would be mostly clear.

The old woman quietly implored him to eat the bread while it was still hot, as she refilled his cup. In the daylight he saw that her hair was heavily laced with gray streaks, and in her eyes was a depth and gentleness he had not seen in the dim light of the kerosene lamps. He nodded and smiled his thanks.

Finishing his meal, he quickly folded the quilt and blanket and rolled up the feather tick. It had been one of the most comfortable, cozy sleeps he had ever had.

His socks, gloves, and jacket were dry and warm, thanks to the stoked-up fire in the pot-bellied stove. He was reluctant to leave, not knowing if the truck would start, but he was anxious to get home.

Reaching in his pocket, Jeremy pulled out several dollars, but a stern shake of the old man's head warned him not to make the offer. Instead, in broken Lakota he expressed his thanks, and the old couple smiled warmly. "I'll be back," he promised as he opened the door onto the bright, glistening morning. They nodded, smiling. He would remember those gentle smiles as long as he lived.

Crisp, cold air was given an edge by a swirling breeze as he paused to pull on his gloves. Leafless short oak trees stood all around the low log house. One of them in front of the house had a thick branch with a deep groove around it, almost as if something had been left hanging from it—something that was now gone.

With his breath billowing in short-lived mists, Jeremy started for the truck. He realized that from the corner of the house he had a clear view of his truck, but if he had stopped it just a few feet further to the south he would not have been able to see the light in the corner window. He shuddered at what the consequences might have been and again acknowledged his gratitude.

The wind had blown away most of the snow. Drifts emanated from clumps of grass, hills, stumps, and trees in long, tapering fingers, but otherwise the prairie was covered only by a thin layer. However, he could still see his own tracks all the way back to the fence. His weight had compressed the snow so much that his footprints appeared like raised white plaster molds.

Pausing after he'd crossed the fence, Jeremy looked back toward the squat log house. It was barely visible among the leafless scrub oaks, hidden amidst the sharp shadows and bright light of the early winter morning. A glance at his watch indicated 8:00.

After unloading the battery from the truck, he installed it again. Then he lifted off the air breather cover and checked the carburetor. He was relieved to see no ice.

In the truck's cab it was warm. Engaging the hand choke, he pumped the accelerator twice and turned the key. The engine was cold, but there was a hopeful cough. Once he pumped the accelerator and turned the key again, the engine sputtered to life. The truck idled roughly at first, and after a minute or two he opened the choke a little. The entire truck vibrated, gradually running more smoothly. After five minutes he turned off the choke and was relieved when the engine kept running, though still a little roughly. Depressing the clutch, he moved the gearshift through the H-pattern to work out the stiffness.

After turning on the heater, he glanced toward the thin grove of oaks. An occasional breeze was sending up swirls of silvery snow, hiding the trees and the house. Nodding a final appreciation in that direction, he carefully released the clutch and started down the road. From the top of a rise some forty yards down the road, he glanced once again at the oak grove but could not see the house. It was well hidden.

Antelope Hills was a welcome sight. Two anxious faces

peered out a window as he pulled into the driveway of his house. The day was bright and virtually cloudless, not a hint that a blizzard had passed through during the night—typical for the northern plains.

After he had finished the story of his sojourn with the old Lakota couple in their log house, Celine, with long black hair in a single braid, quizzed him while she poured coffee and fixed breakfast.

"So who are they?"

"I don't know. I don't think they spoke any English, and I certainly wasn't going to be rude and ask them."

"I know a couple families down around Spring Creek who don't speak any English, but even they have electricity in their houses."

"Well, honey, I didn't see any powerlines to their house from anywhere."

Cora, who had been listening with great interest and a twinkle in her dark eyes, observed, "They have to be somebody's grandma and grandpa."

"I'm sure they are," replied Jeremy. "I think they're the best grandma and grandpa anyone could ask for."

As Celine brought a plate of food to the table, her soft brown eyes still reflected concern.

"You look okay. Do you feel alright?"

"Sure, I'm fine. That feather tick was the most comfortable bed I've ever slept on."

"A feather tick? How do you know it was a feather tick?"

"My grandparents had one. A big one."

She was thoughtful. "Oh, yeah, I think mine had one, too. But I can barely remember it."

"You know what I would like to do?"

"Buy those old folks some groceries," Celine guessed.

Jeremy paused, with a fork full of food in midair. "Yeah! How did you know that?"

Celine smiled coyly. "Well, from how you described the

inside of their house it seems like they're poor. Wouldn't hurt to take them a few things—flour, coffee, bread, sugar, and meat maybe."

Just after noon they finished shopping at Stubben's Market and headed down the Black Pipe Creek road in the sedan. The road was surprisingly free of snow and traffic. About 1:00 they pulled over at the spot where Jeremy had stopped the truck the day before. He pointed at the pasture.

"There are my tracks. All we have to do is follow them."

"You want to go alone?"

"Well, I was hoping you'd come. You know how to speak Lakota better than me."

Celine looked at Cora in the backseat and said, "Come on, make sure your coat is buttoned all the way up, and put on your mittens."

With a bag of groceries in each arm, Jeremy led them across the pasture, remembering how much work it had been to walk in the deep snow. It seemed like a lifetime ago.

Suddenly, he stopped at the dry creek bed, looking frantically right and left. Celine stopped beside him and then saw the frightened look in her husband's eyes. In their seven years of marriage, she had never seen such an anxious look.

"Jeremy, what's wrong?"

Jeremy's confused, frightened eyes darted back and forth, sweeping south and then back north again, squinting in the bright sunlight.

"Jeremy! What's wrong?"

Another moment passed.

"It's not there!"

"What's not there?"

He swallowed and put the bags on the ground, then pointed across the creek. "The house. It was there! Right there!"

Celine stared at the thin grove of scrub oaks. There was no house, only snow-covered ground with tufts and blades of grass poking up here and there.

"Are we at the right spot?"

He looked back toward the sedan and then visually retraced his tracks across the pasture before he looked back at the slight rise and the oak grove.

"Y-yeah," he stammered. "This...this is it, I'm pretty sure, but...." His voice trailed off.

Celine shaded her eyes and looked up and down the creek. "There's nothing anywhere, hon."

Jeremy bolted across the dry creek and up the other side, running to the oak grove and stopping in the middle of it. Eyes wide, he spun around. There was nothing but snow, grass, and leafless oak trees. He was about to run back when he spotted the old gnarled oak with the groove around one branch—the one he had noticed that morning. Trembling, he folded his arms across his stomach and squatted. Celine took Cora by the hand and hurried toward her husband.

"Jeremy! What is it?"

His eyes blinked blankly. "It was right here, Celine, I swear it!" He waved an arm around. "Right here, exactly where we are!"

"There's nothing here, Jeremy."

Cornilius Blue watched as Jeremy twirled the cup of coffee around and around. He had never known his cousin to be so agitated. In his life he had heard a few stories like the one Jeremy had just told, but obviously it was a first time for his younger cousin.

"I want you to go back to that place with me," Jeremy said.

"Sure. When?"

Jeremy glanced at his watch. A week had passed; it was Saturday again, just past 11:00.

"How about now?"

"Okay. What did you do with those groceries?"

"They're at the house. Celine wanted me to leave them out there, but I took the stuff home."

"We'll stop by your house and grab them."

Jeremy studied his cousin's mellow expression for a moment, not comprehending why he didn't seem upset by the story.

Later, they walked the dry creek for nearly a mile in both directions but found no log house. Jeremy pointed out the oak with the deep groove in one of its branches.

"I noticed that when I came out of the house," he explained. "It was like something had been hanging from it."

Cornilius took a deep breath and touched his cousin's shoulder. "Jeremy, tell me something."

Expectation welled up in the younger man's eyes.

"Do you believe that house and those old people were here?"

Jeremy looked around and then back at the groove in the tree branch. "Yes."

"Then, they were here."

"How do you know that?"

"Sometimes the *how* or *why* isn't important, Cousin. Sometimes it's more important just to believe."

"Could I have just gone to sleep in the truck and had a dream? Maybe I was wishing so hard that I had a dream of being warm and cozy by a fire."

Cornilius shrugged. "Could be, but how do you explain your tracks? Celine saw them."

"Maybe I was hallucinating and wandering around in the dark."

"She told me they came straight from the fence to this spot."

Jeremy stared pensively across the bright prairies. "So you believe they were here, those old people?"

"It doesn't matter what I believe. It's only important what you believe. You know, that night was one of the coldest in January. If you had slept in the cab of your truck all night, you could easily have had frostbite. But Celine said you were fine."

"I slept on a feather tick next to a cozy fire. It was the best sleep of my life."

"Then thank those old people by leaving the groceries here."

A breeze dogged their steps all the way to the highway. As he was about to step over the barbed-wire fence, Jeremy thought he heard a gentle voice float by his ear. He paused, but there was nothing more.

Two weeks later Celine brought home a plat map of the early reservation, showing the area just after allotments had been handed out by the Bureau of Indian Affairs around 1900. In the Black Pipe Creek District, near where the Black Pipe Creek road was now, one quarter section was marked "Bear Looks Behind, Allottee 0679."

After the spring thaw as new grasses were beginning to push up, Jeremy and Celine visited an old cemetery a few miles north of Black Pipe School. In one corner were two worn, white marble markers side by side. On the left one was carved "Jacob Bear Looks Behind," and on the right "Cora No Moccasin Bear Looks Behind." In his mind he heard his daughter saying, "They have to be somebody's grandma and grandpa."

Every year afterward, on the anniversary of the blizzard that had stalled him on that lonely road, Jeremy trekked to those two graves at the cemetery, no matter how stormy the weather. He always brought two bowls of stew, two pieces of skillet bread, and two saucers of honey.

And there he would sit for a time, remembering that cold winter night when he had slept the best sleep of his life, cozy by a warm fire.

Nelson and Star

In the old days the Lakota people learned that winter is the season that separates the weak from the strong. In the winter of 1937, on the Rosebud Sioux Indian Reservation, a twelve-year-old boy and his horse discovered that truth.

Nelson Marichal was the oldest boy in a family of eight children—five girls and three boys. Nelson's grandmother, Elizabeth, loved horses. Most Lakotas loved horses; it was a kinship forged in friendship and tempered by adversity on the northern prairies, in that great age when they rode after buffalo and kept their enemies at bay. Such a timeless bond is not easily broken, even under the pressures of reservation life when the Lakota were not completely masters of their own destinies as they once had been.

Grandmother Elizabeth's gift to Nelson of a two-year-old colt in 1935 was made partly to teach him about his Lakota ancestors, who as horsemen once ruled the Plains west of the Missouri River, but mostly with the hope that the horse would help mold the character of her beloved grandson. Little did she know that her hope would turn into reality and Nelson would become a man at the age of twelve.

The colt, named Star, was as devoted to Nelson as Nelson was to the sturdy black horse with the perfect five-point white star on his forehead. The hills and prairies on either side of the Little White River, in the southwestern corner of the reservation, became their conquering ground. There the shared adventures of youth and imagination prepared them both for their winter journey of 1937.

That year the usual early indicators of a hard winter to come—such as horses growing winter hair early, squirrels scurrying furiously to store food, or deer fattening up—were mysteriously absent. Instead, autumn was warm and lazy, simply a continuation of summer. However, Nelson's parents, Charles and Martha, were not completely fooled. Like many among the generations of Lakota who were born and bred on the northern prairies, they knew the fickle whims of weather. The vegetable garden was good, and Martha and her five daughters canned jar after jar to store in the root cellar. A steer had been fattened on corn to be ready for butchering just before the first hard snows in January. And, as usual, Nelson had helped his father lay in a good supply of firewood.

But there was a mean spiritedness in the way the first cold winds of winter swept over the land, driven by low dark clouds that seemed to swat at the earth. The first hard, heavy snows were unleashed in mid-October, along with a bone-chilling cold. Among winter's first victims was the fattened steer, which had fallen into a snow-filled gully and suffocated. By the time Nelson and his father found it, coyotes had taken all but hide and bones.

Then one of the fourteen-hundred-pound draft horses which pulled the plow and hay wagon walked atop the root cellar and fell through. His legs were lacerated by the jars he broke in his panicky attempts to climb out. Although the horse eventually healed, a third of the canned vegetables were spoiled. But the most grievous injury from the root cellar incident was suffered by Nelson's father, who wrenched his back while wrestling log crossbeams to make repairs.

School had started in September, a necessary activity which

Nelson endured with resolute silence. He and two sisters, Adelia and LaVera, walked two miles down a gravel highway to a church which doubled as a classroom for fourteen students. Reasoning that his father's serious injury was a good reason for him to get out of school—so he could haul and split wood, care for thirteen head of cattle, milk two dairy cows, and generally be the man of the family while his father recuperated—Nelson was disappointed when this didn't happen. His parents needed him to walk his sisters to school, he rationalized, because they had a tendency to wander and play along the way.

By November, winter had settled in solidly, and Nelson's father was healing slowly. Nelson and Star worked hard to keep the family's small cattle herd watered and fed. Ice was already forming on the river, a month or two earlier than usual, so Nelson had to keep the watering holes open with an axe—a chore he had to do twice a day on even the coldest days, when the frigid air carried the cracking thud of the axe blade slicing into newly formed ice.

Anticipating a quick recovery, Charles had planned to make the usual monthly trek to town for staples such as flour, sugar, salt, and coffee. But early heavy snows had gathered in the low spots along the winding road, waiting to ambush a buggy or a wagon, and he was still in too much pain to ride a horse.

Consequently, Grandmother Elizabeth quietly suggested that Nelson and Star could make the trip, but new snows continuously fell, and the winds blew, sculpting long, high drifts. Under the best of circumstances, the fifteen-mile trip to town was a man's task, and the deep snow and biting cold made it far too risky for a twelve-year-old boy.

Then at the end of November the weather seemed to relax its heavy hand. A string of balmy days began to melt Charles's resolve against sending a boy on a man's errand. Nelson himself certainly felt equal to the task, knowing that there was no horse anywhere on the reservation as swift and surefooted as Star. The deciding factor was dwindling supplies.

One morning, hobbling painfully, Charles helped his son saddle Star. Food and water for the trip, along with two bags to hold supplies, were hung on the saddle horn, while a heavy rolled-up quilt was tied behind. An envelope containing a list of supplies and cash for their purchase was pinned to the inside of Nelson's shirt. The air was calm and crisp as the land waited stoically in shadow and growing light. Then as the sun broke over the eastern horizon, Nelson and Star began their journey, their passage.

The first perilous obstacle was crossing the river on the ice. After slowly coaxing Star across the ice sheet, Nelson remounted on the opposite bank, and Star eagerly climbed to a hill overlooking the valley. From there Nelson could see a dark knot of figures standing in front of the house, watching his progress. He waved and urged the horse over the ridge, facing the cold, beckoning, snow-covered land as the sun rose higher.

As his father had warned it would be, progress was slow. To prevent Star from floundering in deep snow, they kept to the areas where the snow was shallow. As a result, gaining a mile in the direction of town meant meandering two to three miles over hilltops and ridge backs.

On one ridge, Nelson paused to study the way ahead. His father's orders had been to find the main road quickly and stay on it as much as possible. Shading his eyes from the reflective glare of the sun off the snow, he picked out the fenceline he knew followed the road. But it was another mile or two of twisting trail before they reached it.

There were no tracks on the road, only long fingers of drifted snow—nothing to show that a wagon, an automobile, or even a horse had used it. The first twinge of apprehension settled between Nelson's shoulder blades. But Star's eagerness chased away any doubts, and they pressed on.

The road ran mainly east-west. In places where it lay below the shoulder's outer edge, the roadbed was not visible, and Nelson then followed the north embankment. Where the roadbed rose above the shoulder, the snow on it was not very deep. So for a few miles Nelson and Star alternated between the roadbed and the north embankment.

At the crest of a long, upward slope where the ground was virtually bare, they rested, and Star was able to graze on the blades of buffalo grass piercing the thin, glistening crust of snow. Except for Star's munching and a distant scrill from one of several hawks soaring lazily above, all was quiet. A crisp calmness filled the early morning air.

But this serenity was momentarily broken by a slight sense of foreboding, hiding in a sudden breeze that unexpectedly pounced on Nelson. He suddenly had an urge to return home, but he shook it off by talking to Star.

Nelson reminded himself that he knew the road to town very well. In the spring and early summer when the rains were usually heavy, it was a muddy strip, a dark gash across the prairie. Dusty and dry in late summer and during autumn, it was then in the best condition for wagons to travel. Few people in the area, and hardly any Indians, owned automobiles, although when he had the chance Nelson liked to watch them bounce along, the pop-pop of their engines mingling with the dust pluming up from narrow wheels. Most people journeyed on foot or horseback, and Indian families generally traveled by horse-drawn buggy or wagon.

But now Nelson was utterly alone on the road that looked very different from its appearance in spring, summer, or autumn. Snow and cold changed the land's face, and even his father and Grandmother Elizabeth could not remember a more severe winter during their lives.

In this bleak landscape, nothing else seemed to be moving, although rabbit tracks were all around, and Nelson knew that deer were settling down in the gullies after a night of browsing. It seemed that he and Star, along with the hawks wheeling above, were the only things moving.

Nelson's progress remained steady as long as he stayed on

the road when the snow was shallow and followed the nearest ridgelines when necessary to stay out of deep, crusted snow. Soon he saw a group of low, dark buildings to the north he knew to be the Drucker place, a farm owned by a white family that was halfway between the Marichal place and town.

The sky remained clear and the air cold. Nelson wrapped a long scarf around his head, leaving a slit for his eyes. The scarf kept his head warm, but its main purpose was to keep the relentless glare of the glistening snow from causing snowblindness. Nelson was aware of this winter danger. Exactly as the sun reached the middle of the southern third of the sky, Nelson spotted the outer edges of town where smoke was rising from dark buildings in thin columns. The first half of their trek was nearly finished.

The storekeeper at Auburn's Mercantile was skeptical about Nelson's mission until he saw the list of provisions and the cash in the envelope. While the order was being filled, Nelson took Star to the feed and livery store and bought a half-bucket of shelled corn and watered him.

When Nelson returned for the supplies, the storekeeper surprised him by holding out a note and saying, "Take this note over to Milburn's Café. They'll put a bowl of stew on my account. Eat quickly, though. You want to get going home soon's you can. I'll help you load when you get through."

Nelson was grateful for the stew and the help. The storekeeper arranged the load on either side of the saddle. Then after helping Nelson mount, he reached up to shake his hand.

At the west edge of town, Nelson paused to look back. The buildings were dark blots against the vast landscape of glistening white. Although he had never liked the place, he was curious about things in town, like hard candy and ice cream. It was a place of strange shapes, noises, smells, and people. At the moment he was puzzled about the storekeeper, who had been friendlier to him than anyone in town had ever been.

A sudden shiver of apprehension fluttered up Nelson's back

as the town faded from his awareness, and he looked for his own tracks in the snow to pursue the journey home. Slight gusts of wind had disturbed the loose snow, partially filling the indentations of Star's hoofprints. Then while following Star's tracks in the snow, Nelson suddenly realized something else that had been prodding at the edge of his mind like a soft whisper. With a start he looked up and there, just poking over the southwestern horizon, was a line of gray clouds. During the few moments he watched them, the front widened and rose higher.

An ominous change in the weather was coming—that much was certain. What to do next was not. Nelson could only see two choices—turn back to town and wait it out or keep going. He didn't know where he could wait in town, except at the livery, where he could perhaps bed down in a stall with Star. However, the steadily approaching clouds increased his yearning for home. In a heartbeat Nelson made the decision to continue his journey, urging Star into a fast walk.

Gusts of wind, scouts sent ahead by the winter winds roiling in the big, gray clouds, darted over the cold snowscape. Now and then Nelson was pelted with grains of hard ice, forcing him to turn his head away. Sensing urgency, Star lengthened his stride, his head bobbing in rhythm as the snow crunched beneath his hooves.

Soon the gusts grew more persistent. Nelson knew it was inevitable that the wind would blow steadily sooner or later. Now taller and more massive, the gray clouds began to fill the southwestern quarter of the sky, riding high above the horizon and glaring down on the land.

Keeping his head down and eyes on the trail, Nelson watched the tracks they had left on the way to town now filling in with blowing snow. He suppressed a momentary panic, reminding himself that he knew the road. Although Star's long mane began to whip in the wind and cold began to seep through Nelson's wool overcoat, he tightened the waist belt and tucked his mittens into the sleeves.

Snow began flowing over the land in meandering low, flat currents. As yet nothing was falling from the clouds, but Nelson knew it was only a matter of time until it snowed. He reached down to pat Star's neck—more to reassure himself than the horse.

Each time they gained a ridgeline or a hilltop the wind caught them squarely. And even though Nelson rewrapped the scarf around his neck and pulled the knit cap down over his ears he could still feel the piercing cold. At the top of a windswept ridge, he dismounted and walked to warm himself, remounting when he began to sink in snow over his ankles.

Now the wind was growing steadier from the west, strong enough to make him keep his face turned away from it. In the lee of a south bank of the road, he stopped to let Star rest. To the northwest he saw an encouraging sight—dark spots appearing in the whipped up snow where the Drucker place had to be. They were halfway home.

After resting, Star became more anxious, pawing at the ground. Nelson grabbed the reins and mounted, feeling Star hunker into the wind. Light was fading, both because clouds now filled half the sky and because sunset was not far off. Nelson didn't have a watch and didn't need one to know that darkness was only two to three hours away—not enough time to travel the seven miles home, actually ten to twelve miles because of the twisting trail.

Fear started following along, hiding in the wind's cold breath, prodding and taunting. Nelson began to think he should have stayed in town. A livery stable was more shelter than the open, treeless hills and prairies. He calculated where they would be when darkness fell, as he blew on his mittened hands to keep them warm. In the dark, with the snow already drifted in uneven fingers, it was very difficult to know if they were on the road. Their only chance was his memory of the trail. He was confident he could find his way on a moonless night as long as there were no clouds, something he'd done many times by using the stars as reference points.

In a while, Nelson saw a fenceline with a gate that looked familiar. He reined in Star to study the heavy corner posts, which prompted him to recall that the road would soon turn sharply to the north and then back to the west again. A sense of reassurance surged in him.

But after dismounting to check Star's feet and legs, the feeling was swept away. Nelson was horrified to see that scrapes and gouges covered Star's shins and ankles, wounds that had been inflicted by breaking through the crust of the old snow. Yanking off his mittens, Nelson touched the abrasions tenderly. The horse flinched but stood resolute. A lump rose in the boy's throat. "Star, Star, we have to stay away from the deep snow!"

The horse lowered his head, giving Nelson a push with his nose and pawing the ground.

"Yes! Yes, we need to go, I know."

Sliding his mittens back on, Nelson held up his hands to protect his eyes from the wind as he looked for a safe route around the old encrusted snow. It was no use, he realized. Daylight was fading quickly, and new snow began to fall in small flakes, which, Nelson knew, meant it would come down for a long time.

A different kind of cold feeling settled between his shoulder blades. Darkness was not far off, the snowfall would be heavy before long, and the wind was steady now. Nelson was afraid in a way he had never felt before in his life. His lower lip trembled a little as he led Star to a level spot. Remounting, he gauged his direction in the fading light, leaned into the wind with determination, and gently kicked the horse's sides. Head down, Star pushed courageously into the storm.

Occasional gusts buffeted them, forcing Nelson to tighten the scarf around his neck to keep icy fingers of cold from reaching in. Star plodded on steadily, making the turn north and staying close to the fenceline. In a while Nelson was surprised to feel the wind change direction, then he realized that Star had turned west again. Momentary panic rose until he saw the fence in the vague light. They were still going in the right direction, as far as he could tell.

Although Nelson had been out in moonless nights before when clouds had completely blocked out the stars, it had been in warmer weather, and there had been enough light to make out shapes. On those occasions, the worst that could have happened would have been to get lost. Now he could get lost and freeze to death. The sun was down now, he sensed. Darkness was taking over the land, a cold, heavy blanket covering everything.

Shivering, Nelson tried to remember the road in his mind's eye. He had traveled it many times but never in the winter through drifts and crusted snow. Other times it had not been necessary to pay attention to distances since he had not been in any danger. Consequently, he didn't know how long it took to climb a particular slope or to get from one curve to another. Yet he knew his only chance was to keep seeing the road in his mind's eye, and to guess when to turn or go straight.

Shifting in the saddle, his right knee touched the bag of groceries hanging from the saddle horn. Suddenly, he could see Grandmother Elizabeth rolling out dough to make bread. When she baked bread, it was his job to keep the fire going to maintain steady heat so that her bread would bake evenly. In the summer it always seemed like a hard job because it was uncomfortable to be near a hot stove. But what he wouldn't give now for just a bit of that heat.

Soon, Nelson felt Star moving down a slope. If it was the slope he thought it was, there would be a slight turn to the left and then a sharp bend back to the right. But the left turn didn't come. Instead, Star moved steadily, almost eagerly ahead. Maybe they had made the turn already, and he hadn't realized it, Nelson reasoned. They seemed to be on a level again with the wind blowing from behind his right shoulder. Unless the storm had changed directions, they were heading south—which meant that he had no idea where they were.

Nelson yanked on the reins to stop Star. But to his surprise, the horse yanked back, tossing his head in protest and nearly jerking the reins from Nelson's cold fingers.

"Whoa! Whoa, boy! I think we're lost!"

Star tossed his head again.

Nelson tried to pull the horse back around into the wind. "This way, boy! We have to go back this way!"

The horse responded to the cue and turned, then immediately spun back in the other direction.

Nelson was confused. Never had Star refused the rein. "No! Come on, Star!" Nelson shortened up on the right rein and pulled firmly, bending the horse's neck to the right. Star turned back into the wind, and a tap of Nelson's heels failed to move him.

Nelson kicked a little harder. "Come on, Star!"

Star stood firm.

The cold feeling between Nelson's shoulder blades took his breath away. He struggled to remember which direction they were now facing. North, he thought. The fenceline along the road was no longer a dependable guide since the road was through open pasture here in several places. Nelson dismounted and scraped the snow away with his foot until he exposed a small patch of dirt and gravel, which he felt with his bare hand. At least he knew they were still on the road so he remounted and urged Star on.

Uncharacteristically, the horse refused to move.

"Star…" Nelson started to shout, but the scolding died in his throat. There had to be a reason for the horse's behavior, and Nelson suddenly realized that the cuts and scrapes on Star's legs must be hurting him. He slackened the reins a bit more as he considered what to do and was caught off guard when Star spun to face a different direction and began to walk.

"Whoa!" Nelson yanked on the reins. Star sidestepped, fighting the pull on the reins.

"No! Star! No!" Confusion swirled with the wind as Nelson

lost his sense of direction.

Nelson could feel Star switching his tail, a sure sign he was agitated.

"We have to get home, boy! Behave yourself!"

Star responded with a sharp toss of his head, nearly jerking the reins from Nelson's half-frozen fingers.

"Star!" The shout was also a sob, an expression of panic following on the heels of confusion. Why had he been so eager to ride to town, he wondered. And why hadn't he stayed in town where he would have been safe?

"You can do anything you want, as long as you are willing to put up with what happens afterwards," he suddenly remembered Grandmother Elizabeth saying last summer after he had crawled out too far on the limb of a lightning-split tree jutting over the river and had fallen into the river. Now, in the middle of this snowstorm surrounded by darkness, he finally understood what she had meant. He was lost now because he hadn't assessed all the possible consequences and stayed in town to avoid danger. And he hadn't judged the potential danger because he had been so eager to prove he could handle the ride into town. Unless he found his way somehow in the cold and darkness, he would freeze, and his father would find his body after the storm.

Shivering, Nelson forced the thought out of his mind. There was no one to depend on now, no one to tell him which direction to go, what to do. Desperately, he tried to remember any survival tactics he had been taught. If he could find a thicket, he could crawl into it, cover himself with the heavy quilt, and wait until morning. He could find a slope and ride down it until he found a thicket or even a bank to shelter him from the wind. Yes! That was it! In the deep, narrow gullies that led down to the river there would be thickets of chokecherry, buffaloberry, or plum trees—all good windbreaks. The question was which way to start, and the answer seemed simple enough—circle around, since he wasn't sure what direction he was facing, until he found a slope and then follow it.

With new resolve, Nelson tightened the scarf around his neck and reached down to pat the horse's neck. Then, leaning slightly forward he tapped Star's sides lightly with his heels.

But after two steps forward, Star spun again and turned into the wind.

Nelson's momentary bravado dissolved as the horse continued to act up. Dismounting, Nelson wrapped the reins around a hand and led Star downwind, but the horse refused to budge.

"What's the matter? Star!" Exasperation and panic turned his shout into a high-pitched, unintelligible squawk. A sharp jerk on the reins brought only a jolt of pain to Nelson's right shoulder.

From a few feet away, the horse was only a dark shape. Nelson had a terrifying thought and gripped the reins tighter as he moved up against Star. If Star got away...Star would eventually find his way home by himself if he got away, but he himself would be pitifully lost.

Suddenly, another thought jumped up then ducked out of sight, like a prairie dog at its hole. There was nothing the matter with Star. With a growing realization he let the thought emerge again: Star would eventually find his way home by himself....

Knowingly, Nelson leaned against the horse. "You know the way home. You were trying to tell me," he told Star. In reply, the horse pawed the frozen ground. As if warning them to move, the wind howled and tugged at them. It had gotten much colder just since the sun had gone down. There was no time to lose. Checking the cinch and the two bags of groceries, Nelson nuzzled Star's nose before he remounted. Then with feet firmly in the stirrups, giving the horse as much slack as the reins would allow, he leaned over the horse's neck and spoke affectionately, "Take us home, boy. Take us home."

Immediately, Star turned into the wind, head down, and stepped out into a fast, ground-eating walk. Nelson could see Star's head bobbing but couldn't make out anything beyond that. With one hand on the saddle horn to maintain balance, he moved his hips in rhythm with Star's motion. That way he was more than just a load in the middle of the horse's back, and the movement would help to keep him warm.

Darkness took away any sense of space. At times Nelson could tell they were moving up or down a slope, but he wasn't certain how much distance they were covering. The only certainties were the wind, the stinging snowflakes, the darkness, and the piercing cold. And Star's determination.

Though encouraged by the horse's confidence, a cold uncertainty stayed between Nelson's shoulder blades. The only thing he could do now was to trust in Star.

Star maintained his brisk pace. Once Nelson thought he saw a fence corner appear vaguely then move past his left knee. Only then did he realize that the horse was nowhere near the highway. Doubt began to creep into him, like the persistent cold forcing its way through his coat. What if Star was taking them away from home? If Star became lost, morning's light was a long way off. He felt fear as well as doubt. Still, he thought that at least he was doing something to help himself. Suddenly, he recalled the rattlesnake incident of the previous summer.

While riding up an east-facing slope one morning, he was surprised when Star had abruptly stopped and refused to go. Nelson had spotted a small thicket of chokecherry bushes and had wanted to see if any cherries were ripe. But in spite of Nelson's yells and sharp heel kicks, the horse would not move ahead. Losing patience, he finally dismounted and began walking up the slope. Upon hearing a faint buzz of rattles, he stopped. Soon after spotting the first rattlesnake, he saw the rest of them. Nearly a dozen large snakes were basking in the warm sun. If he had walked among them, he might have been struck by one or more, but Star had seen them or sensed their presence.

He remembered how impressed he had been that Star had known the snakes were there—and how grateful he had been to the horse. This memory renewed his confidence in Star, and he reached down to pat the horse's neck. In response, Star began to trot. Nelson looped the end of the reins over the saddle horn, careful to allow Star plenty of slack.

Then as he began to wave his arms to warm himself, Star suddenly slowed down and seemed to pitch downward. Nelson grabbed for the saddle horn, realizing that Star was picking his way down a very steep incline. They leveled out at the bottom but soon after began to climb another sharp slope. Hearing Star's unshod hooves digging into cold, bare ground, he guessed they were in a ravine or dry creek bed, but he could not remember such a landmark anywhere in the hills east of the river. No matter, he decided, as long as Star knew where they were.

As they reached the top of the slope, Star began trotting once again. He was taking them into the teeth of the wind. Even though Nelson leaned forward, turning slightly away from the wind, an occasional gust seemed to burst through his coat, taking his breath away. In a while he realized his fingers and toes were numb, so he shoved one hand at a time under the opposite armpit and began wiggling all his toes.

Now the darkness and cold seemed to intensify. Snowflakes pelted them mercilessly, driven by a steady wind and hard, angry gusts. Leaving home that morning became only a distant memory, and it seemed to Nelson that all he had ever known was darkness and cold, and the rhythmic movement of the horse beneath him.

As he moved with the horse, he thought about his family. In contrast to this darkness and cold, any chores he was required to do at home seemed almost pleasant. Walking his sisters to school was a task he would happily perform again if the darkness ever went away. And he would be glad to stoke the fire for Grandmother Elizabeth's bread on the hottest summer day without complaining. He fondly remembered the looks on his mother's and father's faces as he had left that morning. In his mother's dark eyes were both pride and worry. And his father's eyes mirrored a happy memory, as if he were remembering a journey from his own boyhood. Nelson longed to be able to see those faces again, and this gave him strength. Star maintained his brisk pace, just as anyone who knew his destination.

The hour was unimportant. Nelson knew time had passed, though he did not know how much. He had never paid much attention to clocks. Mom and Dad and Grandmother would be worried, that much he knew. A feeling of loneliness joined the uncertainty still pushing in between his shoulder blades. Instinctively, to ward it off he touched Star's neck and instantly felt warmth and reassurance. At that moment, home seemed closer.

But the feeling flew into the wind as Star suddenly stopped. Wiping the snow off his eyelashes, Nelson peered into the darkness. Star stood fast. Shivering, Nelson dismounted, careful to keep a hand on the reins, guessing that Star had run up against a barrier of some kind. A barely perceptible shape emerged from the darkness. Leaning forward, he reached out hesitantly, reasoning that if it was something to be afraid of Star would have shied away. His mitten caught on a sharp barb. It was a fence. Not only was there a fence, Star had brought them to a gate. After removing his mittens, Nelson touched the wooden posts and then felt something even colder than the wood—a piece of metal atop a post. His momentary perplexity suddenly dissolved into recognition. "Star!" he shouted into the gale. "I know where we are! You brought us home, Star! You brought us home!"

On a whim, Nelson's father had nailed an empty coffee can to the top of the gatepost after repairing it a few summers ago. The can was an easily recognizable oddity, and several people had subsequently found the Marichal place by being told to come through the gate with the coffee can on the post. That gate was not on the main trail to Nelson's house but was on a knoll overlooking the river, from which the Marichal house could be easily seen in daylight.

Nelson stroked Star, feeling his own tears freeze before they could slide down his face. "You brought us home…you brought us home," he kept repeating in relief and wonder.

Nelson wrestled the gate open, pulled it to one side, and remounted. Then Star took them down a long slope to the river, carefully picking his way across the ice. Now, Nelson barely noticed the piercing cold and the howling wind—or the low branches that, like ghostly hands, tried to pull him out of the saddle.

At the gate to the yard, he saw the kerosene lamp in the window. Dismounting, he led Star up to the front door and knocked. For as long as he lived, he would never forget the look on his father's face as he opened the door. It was the first time his father had ever hugged him. The second time was when he came home from Okinawa in 1945.

Nelson slept until the following noon. The first question out of his mouth was concerning Star.

"I put salve on his legs," said his father. "He's earned all the oats he wants."

"He brought us home. I was lost."

"Yes," replied his father. "But you decided to trust him. That was a brave thing to do. Most men would not have done that."

Grandmother Elizabeth appeared, bringing him a cup of hot coffee. "Few men could have done what you did, Grandson," she added, admiringly.

Even Nelson's sisters smiled at him as they brought him hot, fresh bread.

Later, his mother came and silently kissed his hand, smiling.

In the afternoon, Nelson stumbled out to the barn to check on Star. A warm, throaty nicker greeted him, though words stuck in his own throat. All he could do was lovingly stroke the horse's face. In all of his life he would never have a truer friend.

1965 Continental

▲   Gus Pretty Crow died last spring just when the prairies
▲   were beginning to bloom. Knowing there wouldn't be
▲   many people at the funeral, I wanted to go, but I was too
▲   far away to return home. As it turned out, there were only
▲   fourteen people at the wake and burial, four of them
Gus's children. My father went, as a favor to me.

Gus did not exactly set the world on fire. During my
teenage years, I remember him as a traffic hazard in his
1950 Chevrolet truck, rolling along at twenty miles an
hour on the main highway while everyone else was going
sixty. Four kids, two boys and two girls, would be packed
in that tiny cab, staring out with a detached curiosity as
cars in a hurry—and the rest of the world—passed them
by. However, Gus didn't care what the rest of the world
thought. He was devoted to those kids, who were always
clean and well fed. Their rummage clothes instigated
many a snicker, but if their feelings were hurt no one
could tell. They learned from their dad how to shut out
the rest of the world.

Two years ago on a visit home I saw Gus's oldest son, Jarod
Pretty Crow. While pumping gas, I watched a tribal police car
pull over a pickup truck that had run a stop sign. The young officer who got out of the car was clean-cut, tall, and polite, han-
dling the situation in a thoroughly professional manner. There

was something about him that looked familiar.

As he approached the gas station, I recognized in the man the boy I had seen periodically some years ago. There was nothing pretentious about the young man. He wore the uniform well and didn't strut the way I'd seen many police officers do, young or old, Indian or white. I could tell he didn't take himself too seriously. There was a lot of old Gus in him. Undoubtedly, he was honest, too, like his father had been.

Gus's honesty was one of the few things he had in this world. Although he rarely had more than two quarters rubbing up against each other in his pockets, he was an honest man, something that the county sheriff didn't know and refused to believe. When he finally found out that Gus was honest, he learned the hard way. And the sheriff's life was never the same after that. It all started with a 1965 Lincoln Continental.

Rain was coming down in sheets, pelting the roof of the old frame house and practically drowning out every other noise. It was usual spring weather for the northern plains. At first, no one in the house heard the knocking on the front door, and it was only by accident that Matilda Pretty Crow heard it when she went to the cupboard to put away the supper dishes. "Dad," she said quietly, "someone's knocking."

Gus Pretty Crow, who was then forty-five, looked at his eight-year-old daughter in disbelief. Not that he didn't think that she was telling the truth, since she'd never lied to him before, but he couldn't believe that some fool would be out in such terrible weather.

Folding the month-old magazine he'd been reading, he shuffled to the door. Probably some drunk ranch hand had lost his way in the storm, he surmised.

But standing in the downpour was a natty little man in a trench coat holding a briefcase over his head. Beneath the briefcase was a narrow, dark face with a pencil-thin mustache, bushy eyebrows, and dark, intense eyes.

Gus invited him in, and the man thoughtfully shook the water off his trench coat before he stepped inside.

"Thank you," the man said.

Gus simply stared for a few seconds. In recent memory no white man had ever been that polite to him.

"Somethin' I can help you with?" Gus wheezed, stifling his cigarette cough. Some kind of trouble was the only thing that would bring a white man to Gus's door on a night like this, he thought.

"Yes," replied the man, "my car stalled on the highway, about a hundred yards from your turnoff, and I was wondering if you had a telephone."

Gus chuckled, his weather-beaten face slightly bemused. But there was sympathy in his deep-set dark eyes. "Ain't got no phone," he said, apologetically. "Ain't had one, never. I could give you a ride down to the Polyard ranch, but that damn gumbo road is losing its bottom pretty fast."

The stranger, who was wiping his face with a dapper handkerchief, didn't know from gumbo, but he could tell when a man knew the lay of the land.

"I understand," he said, folding and then putting away the white handkerchief. "I don't suppose you're mechanically inclined?"

"Say what?" By this time all of Gus's family had gathered behind him, sizing up the man in the trench coat.

"Are you good at repairing automobiles?"

Gus's hand jerked toward the front door. "I can keep that ol' truck running, that's 'bout all. Don't know much about them newer cars."

"I'm in a bind," the man persisted politely, "and I would gladly pay you for your time and trouble if you were to assess— to see what might be wrong with my car."

It had been awhile since Gus had had his hands on actual cash money. He scratched his chin. "Yeah, well, don't suppose it would hurt to look."

Though the stranger obviously had never seen the inside of a 1950 Chevrolet truck—this was 1965—as they drove to the highway he noted that it ran very smoothly and was clean.

Out on the main highway, Gus's headlights focused on a large car glistening in the rain. He thought the license plate said New York, but it was hard to tell in the dark. The car was the prettiest Gus had ever seen. But what good is the prettiest car in the world if it can't run, he thought to himself.

"What happened to it?" he asked.

The stranger threw up his hands. "It just stopped running. The headlights went off, the engine quit. After I let it coast to a stop, I tried to start it but couldn't."

"Didja run the battery down?"

"No, the starter wouldn't turn." The stranger looked under the hood with Gus, who pulled out a flashlight from a trouser pocket.

"Turn it over?" It was a request more than a command. There was no sound, not a click, not a whirr.

Gus probed the nooks and crannies in the engine compartment with knowing, experienced eyes. "It's got to be 'lectrical," he concluded. "You have a major break somewhere. Considerin' that your lights don't come on an' the starter don't turn over, it's more than I can fix. All I'd do is get wetter, and it won't do you any good."

"What do you recommend?"

"Well, there's a motel in town. I could give you a ride back. In the mornin' you could give Pete's Garage a call. He's got a wrecker that runs, sometimes."

After locking the big car, they retreated to the cab of Gus's truck. The stranger was quiet and contemplative. "Sir," he began, "I have a problem. I need to reach a town in central Nebraska by noon tomorrow. Does your truck run well enough to do that?"

Gus shrugged. "Truck ain't the problem. I can't leave my kids alone for the time it would take me to drive you."

"Actually, I had something else in mind."

"Yeah?"

"I want to buy your truck."

It was Gus's turn to be contemplative. "Well, I'd sell it to you in a hot minute for cash. Heaven knows I need it for my kids. But this old thing is our only means of getting around," he said, patting the steering wheel.

"I'll gladly give you the car, as well as cash."

"Say what?"

"Cash, a fair price, of course, plus my car."

"It don't run."

"Don't tell me a man like you can't find the source of the problem sooner or later."

"You serious?"

"I've never been more serious in my life."

"D'you know what would happen if I drove down the main street of Cold River in that thing?"

The stranger smiled. "Don't Indians own luxury cars?"

"Nope! Not exactly!"

"I get your drift. However, I must insist—hell, I'm pleading with you. Sell me your truck and I'll give you that 1965 Lincoln Continental."

Gus listened to the rain pounding the cab. Something was nagging at the edge of his thoughts, something like a warning, but yielding to recklessness, he ignored it.

"Truck ain't worth more'n a couple hundred," he said.

From an inside breast pocket, the man pulled out a long, dark wallet, deftly extracting several bills. "You have a title to this, I trust?"

Gus unstrapped the registration from the steering column. "In here," he said, "registration and title."

The man handed over the bills. "Three hundred, and this." Opening his briefcase the man pulled out an envelope, signed a paper it contained, and held it out to Gus. "Title," he said. "Just put your name on the line that says buyer."

"Like I said, you know what kind of trouble this is gonna cause?"

Then in response to Gus's concern, the stranger pulled out a small white card from another pocket. "If that happens, make a phone call to this number."

It was that small white card that ended the law enforcement career of Sheriff Lyle Claxton.

I never saw that 1965 Lincoln Continental until a few years later, having left the reservation the year before Gus acquired it. By the time I saw the car, it was showing the wear and tear of back-country driving and the rambunctiousness of four small kids. Most of its luster was gone, but thanks to Gus's skill with cars it ran smoothly.

My father told me that after the stranger had splashed off into that dark, rainy night with Gus's old truck, Gus fussed over the Lincoln Continental all night long. Only when the first gray light of dawn revealed the eastern horizon and the rain had stopped did Gus see a thick wire that had been cut in two. Touching the bare ends, he got a spark. After wiring the two ends together, he climbed into the driver's seat and turned the key. That engine ran so smoothly Gus could barely hear it. My father always said that seeing Gus in that Lincoln Continental was like seeing an elephant in a canoe. It just didn't fit.

Four pairs of dark brown eyes stared with unabashed curiosity at the mud-spattered car parked just outside the front door, a car nearly as big as their house. "First thing we do," Gus told his family when they looked at the car in disbelief, "is to go to the courthouse so's we can send off to get the title in our name."

It was a statement made out of a hopeful naivete, for as badly as Gus and his kids had been treated at times by some whites, he never lost hope that there was good in white people. Gus usually kept the realist part of himself submerged. Otherwise, it was too hard to live with the condescension and the outright racist remarks that were tossed about with impunity. But his forgiving outlook didn't ease the pain inflicted by words and attitudes. It never had. And despite his optimism, he could already hear the questions and remarks he would have to confront when he showed up with a title to a nearly brand-new 1965 Lincoln Continental.

"Gus, where did you get this?" whined Mildred Laterhousen, a large, round woman who worked in the county treasurer's office. She was taller than Gus and always wore floral print dresses, giving the impression of a walking flower garden. Trouble was, she didn't always smell like flowers, nor was her disposition anywhere as sweet.

Gus repeated the story and laid two dollar bills on the counter because he knew it cost that much to change the name on a car title. Earlier he had gone to the bank to exchange pennies, nickels, and dimes for the two bills.

Mildred turned the title over and over, as if the real story were hidden somewhere on it. When she found nothing suspicious, she consulted another worker, a tall, thin, redheaded woman. The two women side by side, Gus realized, made the number 10.

After reviewing the title, the tall redhead stared at Gus through narrow, watery eyes and then shrugged indifferently. Following her lead, Mildred the flower garden sighed and pulled out forms for Gus to sign and scooped up the two dollars—acting all the time as if simply doing her job was above and beyond the call of duty. "It'll be back in a month," she informed Gus, making it sound like a threat.

Something warned Gus that he should park in the alley behind the grocery store, and after getting supplies, he hightailed it out of town, thankful that the gas gauge showed three-quarters of a tank.

Despite Gus's instructions to his kids not to say anything about their new car, word had gotten around as the last week of school was in progress. It was Gus's habit to drop off the kids at the main entrance to the school, something he couldn't avoid, unless he let them out at the edge of town. People accustomed to seeing the Pretty Crow children piling out of an old Chevrolet pickup truck were dumbfounded to see them stepping out of a shiny Lincoln Continental. To the unspoken questions on perplexed, disbelieving faces, they gave no replies. To the haughty spoken ones, they simply said, "My dad has a new car."

Rural life in the farming and ranching town of Cold Water was considered to be slow-paced. While true in the sense that people didn't move fast unless absolutely necessary, gossip moved near the speed of light. Before school was out on that day, word of the Continental had reached Sheriff Lyle Claxton. His unwieldy family sedan, which doubled as the county police's entire vehicular force, was parked lackadaisically at the intersection just north of the school. No other sheriff before or after Lyle Claxton had ever honed the ability to park lackadaisically. To be sure, he had a gift.

Sheriff Claxton watched the mud-spattered tan and brown Lincoln Continental come and go. Though his own vehicle was only two years old, it certainly didn't have the style and grace of a big luxury car. And there were only a few really expensive cars in Cold Water, none of them owned by Indians. The druggist had a Mercedes, the doctor had one of the new Corvettes, and the widow Merrill had a black Cadillac.

Something about Gus Pretty Crow wearing a battered straw hat and driving a new Lincoln Continental didn't fit in Sheriff Claxton's pecking-order world. He was sure that the dirt-poor Indian could barely afford one tire, let alone the rest of the car. There was a clipboard in the sheriff's office containing lists of every unrecovered stolen vehicle for the past five years. Sheriff Claxton patted his shirt pocket to make sure his reading glasses were there. He had some reading to do.

Gus Pretty Crow knew that Sheriff Claxton was not in a good mood. He'd recognized the sheriff's big gray sedan squatting in the middle of the road on the turnoff from the highway toward his house and had noticed the dark, heavy scowl on Claxton's pale face. The sheriff motioned for Gus Pretty Crow to stop.

Thumbs hooked into his leather gun belt, Sheriff Claxton ambled toward the Lincoln Continental. He was big and heavyset, and ambling was his imitation of gracefulness and coordination. But his size was also his greatest and only virtue as a law enforcement officer. At six feet six inches tall and just under 250 pounds, he was an imposing figure from the front and the back, though not in profile. Seeing him sideways, even the most casual observers realized that the bulk of the sheriff's weight was in between his knees and his armpits.

Sheriff Claxton glanced impatiently at the quartet of small faces staring at him with varying degrees of fear.

"Afternoon, Gus. Traded in your ol' Chevy, didja?"

"Sort of."

"Get a good deal?"

"Got a hell of a deal."

"Want to tell me about it?"

Gus told him the story of the man in a trench coat whose car had stalled on a rainy night.

"He was in a hurry, was he?"

"Like I said, he damn sure wanted to get to someplace in Nebraska."

Sheriff Claxton pulled down his sunglasses and burned a glare into Gus Pretty Crow, mildly irritated when he could see no fear in the Indian's eyes.

"You expect me to believe that, Gus?"

A careful shrug was all that Gus dared to venture.

"All I want's the truth, Gus. You're not holding back the truth from the law are ya, Gus?"

Gus shook his head no.

"Where'd ya get this automobile, Gus?"

"What I told you is the truth."

"Gus, this here automobile is worth more money than you can earn if'n you worked steady for the rest of your natural life. How'd you get it?"

Gus threw caution to the winds.

"You gonna arrest me, Sheriff?"

"Not today, Gus. But I will. I will when I dig up the facts. Course, you can make it easy for both of us and come clean."

Despite the heat from the sheriff's shocking blue eyes, Gus stared off across the prairies—and kept staring even when the sheriff ambled back to his own car and drove away.

"You didn't steal this car, Daddy," Matilda reassured him.

"That's right, my girl. But that ain't what's eatin' at the sheriff. It don't really matter to the sheriff how we got this car. He don't think it's right that we have it."

"Why, Daddy?"

"Oh, I suppose the same reason that Jesus has blue eyes and light brown hair in all them pictures. For some people, things got to be a certain way."

Sheriff Claxton stopped me a time or two, each time using everything he had to be as intimidating as possible, including his shocking blue eyes and his size. I figured out quickly—as most Indians around Cold River did—that if you demonstrated the "proper" behavior the sheriff was satisfied, that is, if you hung your head meekly and acted afraid, he would probably not give you a ticket for whatever offense he was concocting. It was a game for us, and a necessity for Sheriff Claxton. Heaven forbid he should have to do real law enforcement work.

Once, when a drunk cowboy was knocking over temporary outdoor privies with his pickup truck during the annual local rodeo, the good sheriff was nowhere to be found. When buttonholed by a little old lady about the incident, the sheriff gruffly replied, "We were watchin' him the whole time, ma'am." Two weeks later an editorial appeared in the local weekly entitled "Law Enforcement by Observation: A New Tactic." The sheriff did show admirable restraint by not reacting publicly to the tongue-in-cheek rebuke. Of course, some said it was because he couldn't read or that he didn't know how to use the dictionary to figure out all the big words of three letters or more. Sheriff

Claxton did cancel his subscription to the weekly newspaper, however.

The initial buzz over Gus Pretty Crow's new car dissipated quickly. Most folks, Indian and white, chose to believe Gus. For those people who knew him, as incredible as his story might be, it was the truth. Gus was the kind of person to whom unusual things happened. For instance, once when hunting he had been chased up a tree by a white-tailed buck.

But even for the most liberal and tolerant of the residents, there was still something incongruous about Gus driving a new 1965 Lincoln Continental. To Sheriff Claxton, of course, Gus Pretty Crow owning a Lincoln Continental was against the laws of nature. And he was bound and determined to find the truth. But in the end, the truth found Sheriff Claxton.

Over the course of the summer, the sheriff conducted an investigation that would have done the FBI proud. That it failed to turn up the tiniest shred of evidence against Gus Pretty Crow mattered not to the sheriff. To Claxton, it was only a matter of time before he uncovered the one clue that would lead to the unvarnished truth. Meanwhile, he turned the heat up on poor Gus.

By mid-July Gus had a pocketful of traffic citations, mostly warnings. Everyone, including the county magistrate, knew that Gus was the slowest driver in three counties. Sheriff Claxton never intended that Gus would actually have to appear in court, he only wanted to put the screws to him. Still, he couldn't resist citing Gus for reckless endangerment because he drove too slowly. Managing to suppress a grin, the magistrate had thrown out that particular charge, something that only served to strengthen the sheriff's resolve.

At least a dozen times over the summer, the sheriff pulled Gus over for safety checks. Methodically he would ask Gus to turn on the headlights, switch from high to low beam, pump the brakes to make certain the brake lights were working properly, beep the horn, and flip the turn signal lever. After concluding this lawful evaluation, which took at least twenty minutes, the sheriff would study the car's registration as if it were the original King James version of the Bible. And several times the sheriff stopped Gus to check and double check the Lincoln's registration number, or to measure the wear on the tire treads, or to ascertain that Gus's driver's license had not expired.

Gus endured the harassment with the utmost patience. Not that he wasn't seething inside—he simply didn't want to give the sheriff any ammunition. The people in Cold River who saw what was happening assumed that the sheriff was simply harassing Gus—within the limits of the law, of course. But Gus knew otherwise. He knew that Sheriff Claxton was *really* trying to find something wrong—any reason to bring up a real charge in order to impound the Lincoln. So Gus tolerated the frequent stops and always demonstrated the appropriate deferential posturings and responses—until the sheriff tried a new tactic.

Over the Fourth of July, a carnival arrived in town. Gus always stashed away pennies, nickels, and dimes so that he could buy at least one ride for each of his children. And so it was that Jarod, Matilda, Margaret, and Jimmy Pretty Crow were standing in line to ride the Ferris wheel, each clutching coins, when Mildred Laterhousen couldn't find her coin purse.

"I was near the Ferris wheel," she informed the sheriff. "That was the last time I took it out."

When Sheriff Claxton looked in that direction, the first thing he saw was the Pretty Crow children counting out their coins to the roustabout who ran the Ferris wheel. They were all terrified by the time Gus arrived at the jail, where the sheriff had immediately taken them. In the end Mildred Laterhousen found her coin purse without a penny short, and the children were exonerated, but the sheriff had seen a chink in Gus's armor.

Soon afterwards, the Reverend John Wood showed up at Gus's house one evening with disturbing news. Sheriff Claxton had been asking about the welfare of the four Pretty Crow children. Reverend Wood's wife, Karen, was the county social worker, and she knew that the sheriff didn't care a whit for the welfare of any Indian child in the county. Rather, he had implied that he was on the verge of arresting Gus Pretty Crow for grand theft auto and wanted to ensure that his children would not suffer unduly for that action. Although Karen Wood could not be certain of the truthfulness of the sheriff's implication, she was certain of his obsession with Gus Pretty Crow and the Lincoln Continental—as was nearly everyone in the county.

"Clearly," the Reverend Wood said, "he's out to get you any way he can. Perhaps you should simply get rid of the car—unless there is something else you can do."

Gus was at a loss until he remembered the card the natty little man had given him along with the title to the Lincoln. "Reverend," he said, "I need your help."

"Of course. I'll do whatever I can."

The next day Gus knocked on the Reverend Wood's front door with a rumpled business card in hand. "I ain't hardly used a telephone," he said to the reverend. "If'n you'll call this number, I'll work off the charges."

To the reverend's surprise, the mention of Gus's name and the 1965 Lincoln Continental evoked interest at the other end of the line. Someone wanted to talk with Gus himself.

"Yeah," said Gus, "I'm callin' because you said I should do that if there was trouble. Yeah...yeah. No, there's a man here who don't believe me, thinks I stole it. Yeah...the sheriff. Claxton, Lyle Claxton. Yeah? Okay. Thanks."

"What did they tell you?" asked the reverend.

"Not to worry," Gus replied.

On a Monday some weeks later, four men walked into the county courthouse. All were attired in three-piece suits. That in itself was a peculiarity since there were probably no more than two three-piece suits in the entire county. But for years afterward it was not the suits that were the topic of frequent speculative conversation; it was the demeanor of the men who wore them.

The men in three-piece suits cleared out the entire one-story courthouse. No one had ever seen such self-assurance. They were courteous but firm. Their eyes never blinked. Somehow they had induced mindless obedience. All of the seventeen people who worked in the courthouse except one waited on the front lawn, as they had been instructed. The one person who had not been asked to leave was Sheriff Claxton.

After half an hour the four men came back out and politely informed the county's employees that they could return to their desks. It was Mildred Laterhousen who first poked a head hesitantly into Sheriff Claxton's office to ask what had happened. The sheriff, still at his desk staring blankly at a far wall, nodded stiffly in a vague response to her question.

No one ever knew exactly what had transpired between the men in three-piece suits and the sheriff, although everyone was certain something significant had happened. Speculation and gossip ranged from identifying the men as federal agents to aliens from outer space. Through it all the sheriff refused to talk about the incident.

Weeks later, someone noticed that the sheriff had not so much as glanced in the direction of Gus Pretty Crow and the 1965 Lincoln Continental. Indeed, as time went by it seemed that Gus Pretty Crow had ceased to exist so far as Sheriff Claxton was concerned.

The last time I spoke to Gus Pretty Crow was in 1975. By then all of his kids but Jimmy were out of high school. He was still driving the Lincoln Continental. Like most people who had heard about the four men in three-piece suits, I was curious about who they were, and even more curious about what they had done or said to Sheriff Claxton—or what they had threatened to do. Over the years, half the county had questioned the people who had been working in the courthouse that day, none of whom had seen or heard anything.

Of course news of Gus's mysterious phone call surfaced soon

after the incident and only served to fuel speculation and gossip. Although Gus himself had not been in town when the men in three-piece suits had come and thus could not say what they had done, strangely no one ever asked Gus whom he had called and what the conversation had been about that day.

In 1985, Gus Pretty Crow's eyesight failed, and he first went to live with his daughter Matilda and her husband, then with Margaret's family, then with Jarod, and then with Jimmy. I heard there were times when the Pretty Crow children argued over who should keep Gus—not because they *didn't* want to keep him but because they *did*. In my opinion, Gus died a rich man.

As for Sheriff Claxton, he left Cold River after his first and only term of office. Word filtered back that he tried his hand at several jobs, and his wife finally left him. I thought I saw him once on the interstate behind the wheel of a delivery truck. It was hard to tell, though, because he wouldn't look in my direction. Maybe he thought I was Gus.

The Dance House

- As structures go it had not been a thing of beauty—a
- large, nondescript round house made of cottonwood
- logs and a dirt roof, located in a meadow just a long
- stone's throw from the Little White River. But when the
- dance house was burned down in 1910, the small com-

munity of Sicangu Lakota living up and down Grass
Valley was saddened and angry.

It was yet another confusing and heartrending incident in the chain of changes that had plagued the people
for several generations. In fact, the burning of the dance
house actually started in 1887 in connection with a place
and people largely unknown to the Sicangu Lakota of
Grass Valley—in a place called Washington, D.C., by
people called the United States Congress. The instrument of change was something known as the Dawes Act.
Grass Valley was the north-central area of the reservation, the
peaceful lowlands on either side of the lazily meandering Little
White River, still referred to as the Smoking Earth River by many
of the older Sicangu Lakota—those like Rufus Cloud who
remembered the time before there was a reservation.

Rufus often and passionately lamented the passing of the
old days, and regarded the new order and those who ran it with
the utmost suspicion. He had warned that the Bureau of Indian
Affairs had been established to benefit whites, not Indians. As it

turned out, the burning of the dance house was a manifestation of his bone-chilling foresight.

"It is just as I said," he told George Spoon on a cold late autumn morning.

George, old and gray with a face like Black Hills granite, nodded at his slightly younger friend. Thirty-four years ago they had both fought the whites at the Greasy Grass-Little Bighorn-River when Long Hair had been killed. They were young then, but the fire in the belly which had carried them through that terrible two days of fighting had not yet been completely extinguished. There were still battles to be fought, although perhaps not with the gun or the bow and not on the backs of charging war horses. Those days were over, but the war was not over.

It was all about freedom. When the dance house was burned down by the white man who had taken the land on which it stood, another bit of freedom was lost.

"They wanted the Black Hills because the gold was there," said George. "And they frightened old men into signing the paper, so the peace commissioners could say we 'gave' them the Black Hills." The bitterness rose again, like so much bile in the throat, as it did each time they talked of such things—bitterness rising out of the deep, open wound of forced change.

"Now the dance house is gone because they made a law so their own kind could take our land while we are sitting on it," replied Rufus, spitting out the words as if they were rotten meat.

"Perhaps they will dig up my cousin's bones and throw them across the river," George surmised, referring to a relative who had been buried on the same quarter section where the dance house had been. "In two days the *woju wicassa*, "boss farmer," will turn out the longhorn cattle for us to kill and butcher," pointed out George. "The people will come from all over Grass Valley for their meat. That will be a good time to talk. We can talk about the dance house."

"Talking will not give us back the dance house," Rufus added.

"That is so," rejoined George. "But I wonder which is more important—a place to dance or that we can dance at all?"

Rufus pondered the older man's words for several long moments. "Yes," he finally said, "I think you are right. In two days when the people come to the boss farmer's house, we should talk."

Issue day in Grass Valley was a flurry of activity as it was at any issue station on the reservation. Most families came in wagons, some people by horseback, and a hardy few on foot. Fresh meat, rice, beans, sugar, salt, flour, and coffee were doled out by the Bureau of Indian Affairs district agent, known as the boss farmer. Called *woju wicasa* by the Lakota, meaning literally "man who plants," his most important duty, so far as the government was concerned, was to teach the Lakota to be farmers. In that endeavor the district agent at Grass Valley had met with little more than disdain. However, he was popular on issue day, when the cases of food staples were brought out and the Texas longhorns were driven into the slaughter pens.

As something of an acknowledgment to their former lifestyle as horse-mounted buffalo hunters, the Lakota men of Grass Valley were allowed to shoot the longhorns. Each man dispatched one for his family, and the carcass was then dragged by a horse to a spot where the family began the butchering. Then the women would take the paunches down to wash them in the Little White River, laughing and talking as they worked, in eager anticipation of feasting on a delicacy. Sometimes the flour was moldy, weevils were in the rice, or the cattle were so thin that their meat was stringy and tough to chew. That was a part of change—as was the law that said white men could own land on the reservation.

After shooting and butchering the longhorns, several men gathered in a small hollow hidden by leafless sandbar willows. They'd arrived one and two at a time so as not to alert the prying eyes of the boss farmer and his assistants. It was hard to know whom to trust these days.

A small fire was started, and strips of meat hung above the flames. If one of the whites happened along, it would appear that the men were simply cooking. Rufus Cloud squatted and tended the fire, while six others sat cross-legged or stood, every one the image of nonchalance.

"There is nothing we can do to stop this," pointed out Jacob Little Thunder. He gestured at the land in disgust, his old eyes flashing beneath the brim of his hat. "They tell us that this reservation is our land. Yet *their* law gives it away to *their* people. If they give it all away, we will have nothing!"

Heads nodded grimly, anger and confusion swirling about like a whirlwind.

"The boss farmer told Silas Turning Bear that the land taken by whites was left over after all the Lakota were given land," scoffed the youngest of the group, Micah Long Knife. "He said there was enough land for Lakota and whites."

"The way they measured the land," explained Rufus Cloud, "was in small pieces. That way there were more pieces than there were Lakota. If there had been more of us, they would have broken the land into smaller pieces, to make sure there was some left over."

"That is how they did it, that much is easy to see," agreed George Spoon.

"There is something else," warned Rufus Cloud. "Remember when we were given our piece of land? The whites at the agency picked it for us. We could not choose the piece we wanted. With this new law, the whites could pick the piece of leftover land they wanted to live on. That is how the one called John Kincaid got the meadow with the dance house."

"What is this law?" demanded Micah Long Knife.

"They call it 'Dawes,'" answered Rufus Cloud.

"It does not matter what they tell us," observed Simon Broken Robe. "They mean something else. They say they will do one thing, but they do another." The old man sadly shrugged his thin shoulders. "Clearly, nothing here is as we want it to be.

Whites will live close to us, and I hear they are putting a town up on the flats, above the issue house."

"Where did you hear this, Cousin?" wondered George Spoon.

"The Black Robe, the one called Father Kinneson, he said so. He also told me the Black Robes will build one of their holy houses in that new town."

George Spoon snorted derisively. "Hah! They will fool us into going into their holy house, and make us pray the way they do!"

"Don't forget," said Simon Broken Robe, "it was the Black Robes who complained loudest to the government agent about the Ghost Dance."

"Yes," agreed Rufus Cloud. "It was Father Kinneson who spoke against the people coming to the dance house. He said our dancing was insulting his god. Perhaps he told John Kincaid to burn it down."

Jacob Little Thunder sighed and tossed kindling into the fire. "So it is the power of this 'Dawes' which gives our lands to their kind. Perhaps it is that power which helped Kincaid to burn down the dance house. Truly, it seems to be a power we cannot fight."

"Still," mused George Spoon, "my father and others built the dance house. They built it so the people could come together and have a good time in the middle of the bad times. Can we not build another?"

"Will it stand up to the power of 'Dawes' if we do?" wondered Micah Long Knife. "Remember what the Ghost Dancers had to do. They had to hide their dancing in the Badlands and elsewhere, so the government and Black Robes could not see them. If we build a new dance house, perhaps they will use the power of their new law to burn that down, too."

"Perhaps," agreed George Spoon. "The whites seem to think everything we do is somehow against them, or their god. They cannot understand that some things we do are for us, for our peace of mind, to find a little happiness in these strange new times."

"That is true," said Jacob Little Thunder. "The boss farmer here is a shrewd man. He treats us like children, as if we cannot think for ourselves. He is always looking for us to do something wrong. Perhaps we should fool him."

"What do you mean?" asked Rufus Cloud.

"He keeps wanting us to make gardens, to plant in the ground," Little Thunder reminded everyone. "Perhaps we should, some of us. If he thinks we are coming over to his way of thinking, we can build a new dance house somewhere without him knowing it."

"Even so," warned Rufus Cloud, "the people will begin to talk, and there are those among us who are still loafers-around-the-fort. They will run to the boss farmer with the news so they can get something in return."

"We can build it on my land," suggested Jacob Little Thunder. "My family and I will live in it. But it will also be a dance house."

George Spoon smiled at Jacob Little Thunder. "That is a good idea," he said.

Some days later word began to travel up and down Grass Valley that Jacob Little Thunder would need help building a new log house for his family, and he and some of the older men were talking to the boss farmer about plowing and planting. The boss farmer was all smiles. Come spring, he had said, he would have single bottom plows for everyone who wanted them.

Nothing more was said about the burning down of the dance house near the Smoking Earth River, although the people lamented its passing. They watched sadly as the white man Kincaid put up a small frame house, a barn, and fences. Soon, he had hauled away the burned timbers and had plowed up the ground where the dance house had stood. It seemed as if it had never existed.

Built by a few old men in 1892, the dance house had stood

for nearly twenty years. The people must find a way to smile, those old men had said, especially in these hard times. Consequently, they put up the dance house so the people of Grass Valley could come together and dance and smile. The Lakota danced the old dances, talked of the old times, and sometimes they cried. But they did smile, too. Even in the hardest of times, there were things to smile about—mostly aspects of the people's lives.

After the Lakota of Grass Valley had agreed to build a new dance house, Rufus Cloud gathered together a group of stalwart young men, who cut down logs. By the time the first snows fell, all of the logs had been cut and hauled to the site. By early summer work would begin on Jacob Little Thunder's new house.

Winter passed reluctantly. In mid-December, the river froze up early for the season. Hard snows buried the prairies under a blanket of white. The last meat issue for the year had been in October, and up and down Grass Valley men hunted for their families. Fresh deer meat was always a welcome change, especially if the government cattle were thin, as they often were.

By the time February arrived, called the Terrible Moon or month by the old Lakota, food supplies had dwindled. The first meat and staples issue during the Month of Snowblindness, or March to the whites, came none too soon.

Finally, in the Month When the Geese Return, or April, the river ice began to break up. When the people gathered for their regular issues at the boss farmer's house, word had reached some of them about the real reason for Jacob Little Thunder's new house. The people spoke of it guardedly, however, and never when the loaf-around-the-forts were in earshot. No one knew what powers the "Dawes" had. Perhaps it could take Jacob Little Thunder's land away if the boss farmer and the government didn't want a new dance house to be built.

By mid-June, the Month of Ripening Berries, Jacob Little Thunder had finished marking out the place for his new six-sided house. One day men came and honed and notched logs, while postholes were dug some days later.

After he had finished tamping dirt around the last main upright log, Rufus Cloud retreated to the shade of a scrub oak tree, where he politely took a dipper of water from Maggie Little Thunder. "Thank you," he said. "Your new house will have plenty of room for all of your grandchildren, Cousin."

The old woman's eyes sparkled. "For many other little ones as well," she replied softly. "And for anyone else who feels like visiting us."

They both smiled knowingly but said no more. Rufus turned to Jacob, who was cooling off with a damp cloth on his face. "I talked to the boss farmer three days ago," he said. "I asked him how many gardens he has plowed. He shook my hand two times."

"Good. Micah talked to him, too. That will keep him busy and out of the way, teaching everyone how to plow," replied Jacob.

All the people of Grass Valley could talk about on the next issue day was the whites' new town on the flats above the boss farmer's place—to be called Cold River. There was already one building, a mercantile and dry goods store.

"There will be more whites," fretted old man Turning Bear. "I saw two wagonloads along the Smoking Earth River—two families, each with five or six children. They were looking for the markers for something they called 'homestead.'"

"Yes," said Rufus Cloud. "They are all over the prairies. Many will live in the new town, I hear. And some of the whites are bringing cattle herds. They are putting up fences, the wire fences with the points that can slice open someone's hand."

"I saw them picking out spots in the town where they will build their houses. They are like ants," said Jacob Little Thunder. "One of them yelled and shook his fist at me because I drove my horses across his small piece of land."

"One of the first things my father said about them was that they are a very loud people," recalled Rufus Cloud.

"How will we live with them?" asked Micah Long Knife. "Not only are they so loud, but there are so many and they like to tell us what to do!"

"The boss farmer said there will be two stores in the new town, places for us to trade," Silas Turning Bear said, hollowly. "But what can we trade?"

"Twenty years ago," remembered George Spoon, "there were no fences anywhere—and no whites. You could go all the way from the south end of Grass Valley to the north end. My father and the others put up the dance house here because it was in the middle—a day's travel by team and wagon from the south and the north."

"I remember those days," said Silas Turning Bear. "The only whites were two Black Robes. Then the first boss farmer came, the one who froze to death. We had good dances in that old dance house. What little food we had was shared with everyone. We visited, we courted, and mostly we talked about the old days. That dance house helped us to remember the good times in the past, and it gave us good times."

"I wonder if the 'Dawes' can take away our remembering," said Jacob Little Thunder with concern. "What will we have if we cannot remember the stories handed down from the old ones?"

"Is there a power anywhere that can change a heart that does not want to be changed?" asked Rufus Cloud.

"No!" said George Spoon. "They can take our land, make us live in square houses, teach us to plant, cut our hair, send our children away to their schools, and make fun of our God. But all of those things makes remembering even more important. No, we cannot let them change our hearts, because the mind follows the heart. If we stop remembering, we stop being Lakota!"

"That is why the old dance house was good for us," pointed out Silas Turning Bear. "It brought us together, and it helped us to remember."

"If they use the power of 'Dawes' to take away the new dance house, then we will have another," asserted Jacob Little Thunder.

"Or we will dance without one, out in the open under the skies like in the old days," promised Micah Long Knife.

Someone softly cleared a throat, a signal. The group fell silent. Soon young Ezra Left Hand appeared, one of the loaf-around-the-forts—one of those who was skilled in the white man's language and who shamelessly curried favor from the boss farmer. Young Left Hand drove a new buggy, which showed how valuable he was to the boss farmer.

"Uncle," he said to Jacob Little Thunder, "I hear you are building a new house."

Jacob Little Thunder smiled. "So the grasses do talk," he said.

Ezra Left Hand ignored the jibe. "My new team needs a long trip. I will come to see your new house."

"You are welcome to come," replied Jacob Little Thunder. "But I would not want you to hurt your hands. Everyone who comes helps with the work. I am too old to build a house by myself."

The others looked about, suddenly finding birds that were not in the air or ants hiding in the grass. Everyone knew that Ezra Left Hand's palms were soft. It was said his wife did all the work.

Ezra Left Hand tugged at his velvet vest and pulled at the brim of his new hat. "The boss farmer wonders why you are building such a big house," he sniffed. "And I heard that it is round."

"Some of us do not like square houses," countered Jacob Little Thunder. "And I have many relatives who want to visit. It is not polite to make even my brothers-in-law sleep outside."

Ezra Left Hand ignored the chuckles as he turned to leave. "I will come to visit," he said. "I would like to know how it is to sleep in a round house."

Micah Long Knife glared briefly at Ezra Left Hand's back as he departed. "Do you think he knows?"

"He does not," replied Jacob Little Thunder. "He was only looking for something to take back to the boss farmer."

"Still," insisted Micah Long Knife, "it bothers me that the loaf-around-the-fort knows about your new house."

"It does not matter what he knows," Jacob Little Thunder reassured them. "The boss farmer cares more about all the gardens he has plowed and planted. He will not tell the big agent at the agency that there is a new dance house in his district. He does not want to look bad, so he will tell the big agent only about all the gardens he has plowed and planted."

Over twenty wagons were scattered about in the meadow where the Little Thunders' new house stood. The house was located on a slight rise and guarded on the south by a cluster of tall, stately cottonwoods, a short walk from a creek that flowed into the Smoking Earth River. It was a large house, nearly forty feet across, and six-sided with the peak of the roof in the center. The people had been gathering for two days. Many wanted to help the Little Thunders celebrate their new house. For certain, some of them would feel like dancing.

It was early July—the Middle Month or Moon as the Lakota once called it—and the weather was hot. At midmorning the team horses and saddle ponies were already looking for shade, standing in groups and lazily switching at flies with their long tails. Flocks of small children wheeled about, shouting as they ran and played. Some were enduring baths in the cool waters of the creek. A morning meal was being prepared in the shade of the large cottonwoods. Though the men were helping to cook, the women were in charge. Men were gathered around three cooking fires, over which were large black kettles atop sturdy iron grates. A few small skillets surrounded one of the kettles, each heated to quickly cook the Lakota version of sheepherder's bread. George Spoon slowly stirred the savory contents of one of the large kettles containing chunks of stew meat, wild turnips, and dried corn. A few scurrying children paused long enough to look at the delicious-smelling soup, then went on their way, grinning in eager anticipation.

Just as they were about to begin the feast, the muffled rattle of wagon wheels floated on the lazy breeze, and soon a new buggy with two matched bays topped a far rise. Micah Long Knife, standing next to George Spoon, shook his head slowly in disgust. "I knew he would come," he sighed.

George Spoon smiled. "We shall make him an honored guest," he murmured. "We shall feed him until he cannot eat more. Then, tonight we will sing the round dance songs. Left Hand liked the round dances when he was a boy. We shall help him remember."

And so it was that drums pounded far into the night. Round dance after round dance was played. The people honored Ezra Left Hand as if he had single-handedly won the Battle of the Greasy Grass. One unattached young woman after another pulled him into the dancing every time a new round dance song was started.

All in all, no one could remember when the singing and dancing had been so good. The Little Thunders' house was celebrated until even the rafters seemed to sway to the drumbeats. Bitterness over the old dance house was put aside, if only for the evening, and old memories made room for new.

The sun was close to the middle of the sky when Ezra Left Hand sleepily emerged from the tent put up for him near the creek. Before he could speak, a cup of coffee, a bowl of stew, and a large chunk of skillet bread were thrust into his hands.

"Thank you for helping us to celebrate my new house," said Jacob Little Thunder. "The boss farmer is coming tomorrow to look at my garden, I think. I will be sure to tell him how much you danced."

Ezra Left Hand could only wave his hands in protest as a piece of skillet bread filled his mouth.

"Uncle..." he mumbled.

"Your father was a good dancer," Jacob Little Thunder went on. He turned to the others sitting under the cottonwood trees. "His father was a good dancer," he told them, pointing at Ezra Left Hand. "You can see this young man is like his father—as a dancer, I mean."

Ezra Left Hand finally swallowed the bread.

"Uncle," he said, "the boss farmer is coming to see your garden?"

"Yes," the old man said. "I told him there was trouble with the corn. Some bugs, I think."

Ezra Left Hand looked around anxiously. "Tomorrow? Are you certain he is not coming until tomorrow?"

Jacob Little Thunder wrinkled his brow and scratched at his chin, obviously trying to remember something. Then he turned toward George Spoon. "Cousin," he asked, "what day is this?"

"It is the Third Day, I think. What do the whites call it? Winnzzdayf?"

Jacob Little Thunder brightened and turned to Ezra Left Hand. "Then he is coming today," he announced, pleasantly, and looked up at the sun. "In the middle of the day," he said. "He should be here soon."

Ezra Left Hand stared at his uncle once removed, while Rufus Cloud, George Spoon, and the others, who were sitting and sipping coffee in the shade of the cottonwoods, stared off at the rolling hills all around. They knew nothing was wrong with the Little Thunder garden, except that it didn't exist.

"Uncle...," Ezra Left Hand muttered, looking for a place to put down his bowl and cup.

"Eat! There is plenty. Next time you should bring your wife. Does she like to dance?"

"Uncle, I must be going. My wife will wonder where I...."

"Do not worry! We can tell her you were here and that you were good enough to dance with all the young girls last night."

Ezra Left Hand's shoulders sagged. He was, after all, an intelligent young man, a good thinker. Slowly he ambled to the shade and joined the others.

"Uncle," he finally said, after several nervous sips of coffee, "you have a fine new house, and the dancing was good. But the boss farmer does not have to know that your house is also a dance house, or that there was dancing last night. I will not be the one to tell him."

"Those are good words, Nephew," replied Jacob Little Thunder. "The whites think they must know everything. But knowing something is not the same as being wise. I do not think they are a wise people. Better that they should not know everything about us. They take from us what they can see, what they can walk on, what they can carry in their hands. They make laws to help themselves to everything that once was ours, and when all of that is done they will go after what we know and feel. We cannot let them do that. We must keep what makes us truly Lakota. Last night the dancing was one of those things. It reminded you, all of us, how it feels to be Lakota. What is that worth, Nephew? Would you sell that for a new buggy, a new team of horses?"

Ezra Left Hand dropped his gaze to the tufts of grass swaying in the gentle breeze. He shook his head and then whispered, "No, Uncle. I would not. No one should."

Just after midday Ezra Left Hand departed, still worried that the boss farmer would soon arrive to inspect the Little Thunder garden—so worried that he took a seldom used trail. He need not have worried. Of course, the boss farmer was not coming, and in all of his remaining years as district agent for Grass Valley he never once saw the Little Thunder place.

The new dance house replaced the old as a place to be happy, although it did not replace the memories of times past. Whenever the people of Grass Valley came to the Little Thunders' house to dance, they remembered the old days and the traditional ways.

When the Grasses Talk

▲ During my youth, one of my favorite places was a bluff
▲ overlooking the Little White River, which my grandfather
▲ always referred to as the Smoking Earth River, sometimes
▲ correcting me when I called it the Little White River. That
▲ bluff was about eighty feet above the water, at a bend
that turned northeastward. The Little White River flowed
north and eventually emptied into the Big White River.
My grandmother's half section was on the flats to the
south and above the river, with the northeastern corner a
long stone's throw from that bluff.

The bluff was gray shale, crumbly, and hard to climb,
which I didn't often do. Instead, I preferred to sit on the
edge of it looking up and down the valley for miles. The
river was a bright ribbon on the floor of the wide valley.
For some strange reason, on cloudy days it seemed even
brighter than it did under clear skies, taking on a silvery
appearance.

The valley itself also looked different from day to day, and from
season to season. Although my favorite season is winter, I was
always awestruck by the colors in late September and early
October when cottonwood, oak, ash, elm, chokecherry, plum,
and willow leaves turned yellow, red, and purple. Sitting on the
bluff, I would admire the splashes of color against the yellow
grasses of the valley floor, and listen to the grouse drumming

and dancing on the prairies behind me. During such moments, I felt so alive and imagined even the trees were dancing. How can anything not dance when wearing so many colors, I would wonder. That portion of the Little White River Valley, several miles in either direction from that bluff, was my playground, my proving ground. As a boy I wandered over about 150 square miles, mostly on foot, sometimes on horseback, and always with at least three dogs.

In early August of this year, I spent a day on the remaining quarter section of my grandmother's land, crossing an old fence to walk to the bluff, where I sat with my feet over the edge. As a hot sun beat down, with a playful breeze providing some relief, I turned loose my boyhood memories—wave after wave of them, like Lakota warriors riding over the crest of a hill. Yet, as I lost myself in those memories, tugged by one and then another, there was one more persistent than the others. Perhaps it was because my gaze had settled on a spot on the valley floor where at age six I first noticed something unusual.

That year, late spring was wet, and the grass on the prairies was thick and tall—already knee high to a grown man in the Little White River Valley. Sitting on the bluff one day, I noticed something curious across the river—three ovals where the grass was noticeably greener, as if a giant hand had drawn dots on the earth. The circles were in a triangular formation; two were in a straight north-south line, and the third was to the east of them.

I thought that I knew every landmark in the valley from the vantage point of that bluff. Yet here were three circles in the grass that seemed to have appeared overnight—something eerie yet intriguing. My curiosity soon overwhelmed my apprehension, and I waded across the river toward the grassy meadow with the circles. At ground level the circles were not easy to see until I walked among them, discovering that they were about fifteen feet in diameter and darker green than the surrounding grass. Going from circle to circle, I played a sort of connecting-the-dots game.

That evening I revealed the discovery to my grandparents. My grandmother smiled a little as she finished preparing supper, while my grandfather nodded knowingly. During the meal he finally cleared his throat to speak.

"The last time I saw those circles was before you were born," he informed me.

I was disappointed. I thought I had been the first to see the strange green circles. "You saw them, too?" I asked.

"Seven years ago. It was a spring and summer with much rain, like now."

"I can show them to you tomorrow. What are they?"

"Lodge circles."

"Lodge circles? What are those?"

"Places where lodges once stood."

My disappointment was washed away by renewed curiosity. "What lodges? Whose lodges?"

My grandfather smiled. "Three," he replied, "but I do not know who put them there."

"When?" I persisted.

"Long ago," came the patient reply.

"How do you know?"

"The green grass. It grows where the picket pins from the lodges were pounded into the ground."

I knew about lodges and about picket pins, which were short, thick stakes usually made of ash or chokecherry that were pounded into the ground to hold down the edges of lodge covers.

"I did not see picket pins in the grass," I said.

"They rotted long ago and then fed the earth. The earth swallowed up the decayed wood. The grass is green where the picket pins were once pounded into the ground."

I was confused. "What happened to the lodges?"

"Taken down and loaded on drag poles behind a horse," my grandfather speculated.

"How do you know there were horses?"

"The size of the lodges. They are large," he pointed out, holding out his arms wide. "Before horses came to our people long ago, the lodges were the same, only smaller. They were small because they were carried by dogs. Dogs cannot carry big loads like horses can."

"There was a time when our people did not have horses?"

"Yes. Very long ago."

I began to imagine a time when horses were not around. We had horses—two teams of big horses to pull the wagon and the plow, and two smaller riding horses. In a moment my thoughts returned to the lodge circles.

"Three lodges stood down there close to the river?"

"Yes," the old man replied after sipping his wild peppermint tea.

"The people who put them there, who were they?"

He smiled. "People with horses and three lodges," he said.

"A large family, maybe three families," added my grandmother, who had been listening with great interest.

"Families? How do you know that?"

"The lodges," she replied. "Men out hunting or going somewhere to make war do not travel with lodges. A group with women and children take along lodges."

My other questions were quietly waved aside for the moment because there were chores to do. I had to haul water from the spring to the house and fill the wood bin next to the cooking stove.

"Tomorrow, we will go to the river," promised my grandfather. "And we will talk about the lodge circles."

Being an impatient six year old, the night seemed much too long. Finally, the first hint of gray dawn light assured me that tomorrow had come, and I left my bed. It was one of the very rare mornings when I was up before my grandparents.

I built a fire in the cooking stove and put on a pot of water to make coffee, wondering if the grass circles would still be there. Somehow I refrained from mentioning them as the morning wore on, although my impatient glances toward the bluff certainly left no doubt as to what was on my mind.

At midmorning, when I had almost given up hope that my grandfather would go with me to the river and was nearly ready to go alone, I saw him grab his walking stick. Before long we were on the bluff, and I was overjoyed to see the green circles in the grass.

To my delight, there was something in my grandfather's demeanor that told me he also was excited to see the circles. I realized he was my connection to the land and to the past through all the stories he knew and loved to tell. If anyone knew anything about the circles in the grass, it would be him, and I was impatient to hear his story.

We sat on the edge of the bluff as a breeze ruffled our hair. The air was cool with a promise of rain.

"What do you see from here, Grandson?" he began.

I was elated. That was the question, in one form or another, he always asked when he began to tell stories about the past.

I looked up and down the valley. "The river," I replied. "Trees, hills, the meadow."

"Is that all?"

"Yes."

"What about those two deer bedded down in that draw there?" he said, pointing. "What about those hawks building a nest in that tall cottonwood? Or that coyote on that hillside over there?" I had not noticed any of those animals, and decided I would never again believe the old man if he complained that his eyesight was getting bad, which he did now and then.

"And there is much we cannot see," he went on. "The insects in the grass, anthills, mole tunnels, meadowlark nests...."

Finally, he pointed to the circles in the grass. "Six, seven years ago they were there, just as they are now. The years in between were dry with not much rain. So the grasses could not tell their story."

"What?" I stared at the tufts of grass nearby. I knew they couldn't talk, though I had heard the wind whisper through blades of grass now and then.

"Grandpa," I ventured resolutely, "I never heard grasses talk."

"That is true, Grandson. They do not talk like you and me, but sometimes they have stories to tell. Everything has a story to tell, if you know how to listen."

My attention was fixed on the circles in the grass across the river. "What do the grasses say?" I asked.

"They say that someone was there." The old man pointed his walking stick down at the circles. "Your grandmother was right. It was a family, perhaps a large one. Or maybe it was three families. Whoever they were, they pitched their lodges there."

He lifted his stick toward a low butte on the opposite side of the valley, one I had climbed up a few times. "From there," the old man continued, "a person can see a long way off in all directions. From here, too, where we are."

Suddenly, I began to realize that the grasses were talking through my grandfather.

"Long ago, when those people came here and pitched their lodges, they picked a very good spot. I think that one of them climbed that butte, another came up to this bluff—boys or maybe young men. From those two places, they could keep watch."

"For enemies?"

"Yes, for enemies. If any came, a warning signal of some kind, perhaps a fire arrow, could be sent."

One of the dogs accompanying us perked up her ears and wagged her tail. There was a soft rustling in the grass, and without turning I knew it was my grandmother. We waited while she seated herself next to me and took a deep breath. It was as if she had been listening to the conversation all along.

"If they were here in cold weather, that is the best spot to pitch lodges," she said. "There is good shelter down there from the wind. There's dry wood all over, too, for the fires to cook with and keep warm. And grass for their horses. If it was winter, there is young cottonwood all over, and you know how horses like to eat young cottonwood bark."

"Grandma, have you seen those before?" I asked, pointing to the circles in the grass.

"Yes, many times since I was a young girl. This is my mother's land," she said, pointing back toward the half section on which we lived. "She and her sister inherited it, after my grandfather died. So I have lived here since I was just a girl. Every year there is good rain those circles have appeared."

I felt goosebumps on my arms, and a chill went through me as I realized I was experiencing the same phenomenon my grandmother had experienced during her youth, making my connection with her even stronger.

"Who were those people, Grandma?" I asked, anxious to see more through her eyes.

She shook her head slightly while shooing away gnats with her scarf. Draping the scarf over her neck, she tugged at her two long, gray braids before she replied.

"No one knows," she said, a little sadly I thought. "Over the years your grandfather and I have talked about that. We know they had horses, as your grandfather said last night, because the three lodges were big. Since there were three, perhaps there were twelve people, maybe more."

"Were they all related?" I wondered.

"Yes, I think so," she said, waving at the pesky gnats again.

"What were they doing? Where were they going?"

"They had to be traveling north or south, because they were following the river," pointed out my grandfather. "Perhaps they were a family going to visit relatives somewhere, and they camped here for the night."

"Or they might have been banished," said my grandmother.

"Banished?"

"Yes," she affirmed. "One of them, a son or a father, might have done something very bad. Perhaps they killed one of their own people. For that they would have been driven out, or banished. Sometimes in the old days when that happened, a man's entire family went with him."

"Where to?"

"Anywhere, everywhere, so long as they stayed away from the rest of the people."

"That sounds lonely."

"It was. So if the people who came here were banished, they might have stayed here for a few days—maybe even a month or two."

"Yes," said my grandfather. "The deer have always been plentiful around here. Only once, during the time when the winds blew and the land turned to dust, the deer were few. But when they were here the hunting was good. Back then there were bison here, too. This is a good spot to stay, to hunt, and to make meat."

"So you think they stayed a long time, down there?"

"We do not know for sure," said the old man. "But we do know they left in a hurry. They fled from something, or someone."

"How do you know that, Grandpa?" I asked in amazement.

"They left the picket pins behind in the ground. That means they took down their lodges in a hurry. They had to move fast to get away."

"From what?"

"Enemies, perhaps," said my grandmother. "Maybe a grass fire or a flood—something that was dangerous."

As I stared down at the circles in the grass again, I could see women pulling down the lodge covers and dismantling lodge poles while men gathered their bows and arrows and all the horses. In my vivid imagination, the people had long black hair and brown skin, and were dressed in tanned shirts, dresses, and sturdy elk hide moccasins. They worked quickly, folding the lodge covers and the dew liners, loading bundles, tying rawhide cases of clothing and food onto drag poles. There were two or three small children, I imagined, as well as two sentinels, one on the far low butte and the other on the bluff where we sat, who galloped their horses to rejoin the group as it hurried away to the northeast. In my mind they escaped from whatever enemy was approaching, and although I let them fade away, I would never forget them.

"Were they our people?" I questioned, wanting to know more.

My grandfather stared down into the valley as he slowly shook his head. "I do not know. Perhaps," he allowed. "They could have been Cheyenne, they were here before us. Or maybe they were Kiowa or Arikara."

"I thought the Kiowa and Arikara were our enemies. What would they be doing in our country?"

"The Kiowa and the Cheyenne were here in the prairie country before our people came," pointed out my grandmother. "The Cheyenne became our friends. The Kiowa moved away south because we were too many for them. The people who put up those lodges down there could have been here long before our people, the Lakota. It is hard to know for sure."

Then it struck me that there was only one thing of importance. "*Someone* was down there long ago," I said.

"That is true. So I do not think it matters if we know what people they were," said my grandfather. Again, he pointed his walking stick toward the circles in the grass. "They were there. We will never know for sure who they were, their names, what language they spoke, or why they were there. But they were there. So when the grasses talk, you must listen and hear. They will tell you many things. But the most important thing they will tell you is this: the land is old. Very, very old. Older than anyone can know and remember. When your grandmother and I are gone, perhaps you will be the only one to know the story of the circles in the grass. And after you are gone, who will know?"

I shook my head.

"The land will know. And it will tell the stories, if any two-leggeds know how to listen."

Grandfather was right. And I never forgot what he said that day about listening to the grasses.

That year the circles were clearly visible until midsummer. Then they faded as the grass on the riverbottom grew thicker and the rains did not come as often. By autumn, I could not see them any longer. But I had seen those circles. I had heard the grasses talk. I knew part of the story they knew.

The following year, when I was seven, they did not appear. The year after that I was taken away to a government school and didn't return until the following summer. One summer, long after my grandparents had moved off the land, I did see the circles again, but I haven't seen them since.

Perhaps I haven't been there at the right time, or maybe the nutrients provided by the decaying picket pins have weakened, and there will never again be circles where the grass is greener. In a sense, it doesn't matter because I know that they were there, and I know the story they had to tell.

Now, no one lives on my grandmother's land. All that is left of it is a quarter section, which is leased to a nearby rancher who runs cattle on it. I can't say what kind of connection he has with the land, beyond its significance to him as a commodity, a way to fatten his cattle.

The grasses have more stories to tell since the log house my grandfather built was torn down and hauled away. There are still slight depressions in the ground where the four heavy corner posts were. A few yards away are the scattered, gray remains of a cottonwood tree he planted. Some of the pieces are in the depression where the root cellar was. About fifty or sixty yards away, are a few bleached rib bones of a draft mare, which also tell a story. The horse fell on her back in a deep drift covering a narrow gully and, unable to extricate herself, probably suffocated before she froze to death. My grandfather dragged what the coyotes had left back to the straw barn.

Two hundred yards to the northwest, in a deep gully guarded by oak, elm, and ash trees, the water still seeps up out of the ground—the coldest, sweetest water I have ever tasted. There my grandfather had dug a catch well and lined it with stones. The spring water seeped in and filled the well, and in it we dipped our buckets to fill the water barrel. Forty-four years later the silt has filled in the well, but I know the stones are still there. If anyone were to remove the silt, my grandfather's catch well would function again—of course that individual would have to know exactly where the well was, would have to know the stories.

This past August I wandered over my grandmother's land for two days, with memories and stories following me, swirling in my mind like a whirlwind. My grandparents are gone now, but as I stood on the site where the log house once was, their presence was as real as anything that I could see, hear, or touch. Because they had been there. They are part of the stories now, mingling with all the others the land knows. Perhaps they now know who it was that came to that valley and pitched three lodges on the riverbottom.

On that visit, the circles in the grass were not visible—perhaps it was too late in the summer. But they had been there, and their story would live on. I don't know if those lodge circles will ever appear again. But I will go to that bluff and look for them, as often as I can, and listen to what the grasses have to say.

Pride

▲   That black-and-white horse grew up under my nose, but
▲   I really didn't notice him until he was four and I was ten.
▲   Yet I haven't forgotten him, and I never will.

▲   My grandfather drove him and the other horses into
▲   a pen one autumn evening in 1947. The others, except
for one saddle horse, were tall, stout draft horses with
barrel chests and big, wide hooves. Gentle in spite of
their size, they pulled the plow, the mower, and the
wagon. One of them, a patient old mare named Queen,
had taught me how to ride. The saddle horse was a hot-
blooded bay that only grown men could ride. I had rid-
den him for the first time just after my tenth birthday. As
a rider, as far as I was concerned, I was more than a boy.

The bay at least had a purpose. The paint, as yet on
that autumn evening, had none.

I climbed the corral to look at him. He was gaunt, his hooves in
need of trimming, his mane tangled and uneven, and his tail
nearly touched the ground. Losing interest, I soon went to help
my grandfather corner the bay. Now, that was a good, fast horse.

The paint slipped out of my awareness until a few days later,
when my grandfather said something about selling him. But he
was worried that the horse wouldn't be worth much because his
right eye was stone blind, something I hadn't noticed. My grandfather speculated that he might have injured it in the thick scrub

oak along the river, on a fence, or maybe fighting with one of the other horses. Although it was not plainly noticeable, the injury was yet another mark against him in my mind.

Early the next morning my grandfather sent me to look for the paint. Astride the bay, I probed the draws along the river where he usually hid out. I found him, chased him out of some tangled plum thickets, and maneuvered him toward home. Up on a flat he kicked up his heels and changed his life, along with my idea of what a good horse was. He turned east toward a large, open section of pasture. I nudged the bay confidently into a gallop, intending to circle that wily paint and point him in the right direction.

The bay easily drew close, but with a snort the paint kicked up his heels again, flattened out into a smooth gallop, and sped away from us. This was a challenge the bay and I felt compelled to accept. I grinned and crouched low over the bay's neck and drummed my heels into his sides. He hit top speed in just a few strides, and I knew we'd catch that skinny runaway. However, soon my confidence turned to anger, then astonishment when the paint kept widening the distance between us.

At home a couple of hours later, confused and a little ashamed, the bay and I managed to maneuver that runaway into the pen. After cooling off the tired bay, I went to the corral to glare at the paint. He sized me up with his one good eye, snorted, and gracefully singlefooted to the other side of the pen.

My grandfather listened to the news of the morning's incident without a word, but I noticed a twinkle in his eye. Still stinging from the embarrassment of being shown up by that skinny, half-blind horse, I was hoping that the old man would waste no time getting rid of him. That evening, though, he asked me to take a letter to the mailbox on the highway, a letter for John Chase, his nephew. John was twenty and a good rider and I began to wonder what the old man had in mind. Deep down inside I knew it had something to do with that paint, but I wasn't sure if that was good.

A week later, John came. By then we had managed to put a halter on the paint, and he was beginning to respond decently to a lead rope. That is, I helped to catch the horse, and my grandfather worked with him after that. I wasn't sure what a half-blind horse could do, and I might have been just a little afraid of him. I watched as the old man trimmed his mane and thinned out his long tail. He was still gaunt, but he didn't look as wild after that.

John had learned the Indian way of taming a horse from his father and grandfather, a gentle but persistent method done in steps. First, he talked to the horse soothingly while he rubbed, scratched, and patted the horse's neck, chest, sides, front legs, and then—amazingly—the back legs. If the paint showed any sign of nervousness, John stopped where he was but never backed off. And he never ceased talking in a soft, soothing voice.

I lost track of time as I watched the man work. He made no sudden movements, and his voice was low and matter-of-fact, as if carrying on a conversation with an old friend. At some point I noticed a calm, almost sleepy look in the paint's one good eye. I held my breath, though, when John jumped up and draped himself over the horse's back just behind the withers. Amazingly, the paint stood calmly, totally trusting. After a few more soothing words, John was suddenly sitting astride the horse, and the paint seemed more concerned about the flies circling his head than with the man on his back. Before I knew it he responded to some cue or touch from John and started walking, and soon trotting, inside the corral.

My grandfather had told me stories about how the Lakota of the past tamed and trained their horses, but I didn't think there was any connection with present-day methods. However, here was John riding bareback, and the paint was moving quite willingly. Perhaps the most astonishing thing was when he stopped, praised the horse lavishly, slid off, and then proceeded to pick up each of the horse's feet one at a time—all without the paint flinching or showing any nervousness.

Then when John motioned toward me my heart pounded

unexpectedly. He wanted me to step into the corral. My hesitancy must have been obvious to my grandfather, who laid a reassuring hand on my shoulder.

"Go in," he said, quietly. "Move slow, walk slow. Walk over to John, stand beside him."

The paint seemed half asleep, but I still was nervous.

"If you are afraid, the horse will know it. There is nothing to be afraid of. The horse will not hurt you. Go on," my grandfather insisted gently.

Taking a deep breath, I climbed over the wooden rail. Then, inhaling deeply again, I took hesitant steps toward John. The paint looked at me with his good eye and switched at flies with his tail. I stopped next to John, proud of myself for not having scared the horse.

"In the old days our people had no corrals," John informed me. "The best way to keep horses near the village was to teach them not to be afraid of people. Colts were handled and talked to right after they were born. Sometimes they were kept in the tipis." He patted the paint's thin neck. "This is a good horse," he said. "Strong. He has a good heart. If he likes you, he will always be your friend. Now, walk up to him, slowly. Rub his neck, his shoulders, sides. Talk to him. Lean close to his head, feel the warm breath from his nostrils, let him feel yours." I did all these things and I will never forget the experience.

Today I think it was John Chase and the paint who taught me not to be afraid. When I think back on that moment in the corral and the paint's soft nose against my cheek, I remember how John's voice carried the wisdom of all those who had mixed their breaths with horses. When I felt the paint's breath mingling with mine, he pulled me inside of him, past the skinny ribs and the blind eye, to his heart. From that moment on, he had mine.

Weeks passed, John came and went several times, and the paint was becoming quite a riding horse. Meanwhile, my grandparents started their harvest, and we took a wagonload of corn, potatoes, cabbage, and peas to town, which was our means of making a living. Though my grandmother got some money for leasing her pastureland to a nearby white rancher, the produce from the garden was traded for staple items such as coffee, sugar, flour, and salt. The trip to town and back took an entire day, from dawn to sunset. For many Lakota boys my age, a foray into town was exciting but not for me. The open prairies were much more fascinating to me than a collection of buildings and the smell of coal smoke. Besides, I didn't speak English that well then, but the prairies spoke the language of the heart, the same language spoken by the paint horse.

Then, it started.

One Sunday after church—my grandmother was an Episcopalian—someone arranged a horse race—not an unusual event since someone always had a horse he thought was faster than anything on four legs. Racing horses was one of the good activities left over from the old days, my grandfather said. It was one way to be truly Lakota again, at least for as long as the race lasted.

My grandfather entered both the bay and the paint in this race, and we won—that is, John and the paint finished a good stone's throw ahead of me and the bay, while I managed to finish three lengths ahead of the third-place horse. Life for the paint and me was never the same after that.

Following the race, my grandfather persistently refused all offers for the paint. By now he had named him Rock. John continued to work with him, and eventually we took him to the annual rodeo in town.

At the rodeo, that half-blind horse caused a stir when he won two races in two days. As a result, my grandparents were a new canvas tent and fifty dollars richer.

A couple of white ranchers were especially stirred up since Rock had beaten their best horses. They talked to my grandfather about a three-horse match race. It was a matter of pride, they said. Finally, the old man agreed to the race but didn't want any betting.

Word spread quickly, and by the time the race was to begin the three small stands at the rodeo grounds were packed. I was nervous as I helped John lead Rock to the starting line. There were hard stares and sneers on the faces of many of the whites. For a moment something inside of me actually hoped that Rock would lose. I sensed there was something more than a horse race happening, but I couldn't make sense of it—not until years later.

When the horses were ready to begin the race, John gave me a smile, and Rock exploded from the starting line. He led all the way and was still pulling away from the other two horses when he crossed the finish line. The only noise was a few shouts and war whoops from the Indians gathered near the stands.

Autumn came and went. We finished the harvest, and my mother and father returned from Nebraska, where they had been following the crops—picking potatoes and shocking wheat. My father had been in the war in the Pacific and had won a medal at Okinawa. He was a quiet man given to staring off into the distances, a characteristic resulting from the war, my mother said.

After my parents returned, my father and grandfather worked on the house, rechinking cracks between the logs and fixing windows for the winter. I had to attend school, and although some days I rode Rock to school most of the time I walked or ran the three miles. Even though I put up with classes, as I saw it, school was a waste of time. Most of the other students were white and talked too fast for me to understand them.

Away from school I spent a lot of time with Rock—time I will never forget. Rock and me and three hounds roamed the hills, draws, and flatlands for miles around our place.

One morning in December my grandfather looked at the sky and told me to ride Rock to school. By one o'clock that afternoon the teacher sent us home when large snowflakes began falling from the low, dark clouds. Before I was halfway home, the blizzard hit with a vengeance.

Rock and I found shelter in a scrub oak thicket, hoping to

wait out the storm, but standing only made us colder so we started riding through the snow. By now the snow was falling so fast we couldn't see, but Rock put his head down and walked easily, and something about the way he carried himself put me at ease. I knew we were close to home when we went up a long slope, crossed a deep gully, and stopped at the barn made out of hay. From there I could see the dim glow of the kerosene lamp in the front window of the house.

After that winter day, Rock became my dream maker.

In the spring I turned eleven. Another garden was planted as we shook off the long, cold winter. My father and grandfather talked about racing the bay and Rock, saying I would be the rider.

Soon we laid out a course on the prairie west of our house, where Rock and I practiced long and hard. The pounding of his driving hooves became a part of me as I learned to handle the tremendous energy and heart of that horse. Rock seemed to sense that there was a purpose in such practice runs. Every dawn he would meet me at the corral rail and scratch at the ground with his hoof then nicker and prance until I gave him his morning run. Slowly, we became a team, and more. We became friends.

It was a summer of dreams. By the first of July we had won three races and set our sights on a Fourth of July rodeo in Fort Pierre.

Since my father's old Chevrolet had broken down we headed north in the wagon. It took the four of us—my father, grandfather, John, and me—three days to travel the ninety miles to the rodeo grounds. For most of the trip, Rock was on a short lead behind the wagon. Although I rode him a little, we wanted him to be as fresh as possible for the rodeo events. When he was on the lead, I sat in the back of the wagon and talked to him.

At night we made camp, picketing all the horses around the wagon. Then John and I listened as my father and the old man told stories while we all sipped coffee and watched the orange moon rise then turn gray-blue. At such moments I was glad to be who I was.

In Fort Pierre, my father and grandfather spent every bit of cash they had to pay entry fees. There were six qualifying races plus a final, and the first place prize was one hundred dollars.

The track was oval, a little rough, and just over half a mile long. For the qualifying heat, I was instructed to hold Rock back but to make sure he placed at least third. However, that paint didn't know how to lose. The best I could do was make it look like he barely eked out a win.

Right up to the moments before the final race John kept talking to me, keeping me calm and laying out the race. I was to hold Rock back until after the first turn, then let him have his head.

Soon, it was time for the final race. Each horse's rider and owner was introduced to the huge crowd over a loudspeaker. I had never seen so many whites in one place at one time. As each horse came up to the starting line, a smattering of applause and cheers followed each announcement. When the name of White Feather Tail was haltingly read over the loudspeaker, there was no applause, and I thought I heard some laughter. But John reassuringly patted my leg and reached up to shake my hand.

Moments later, when the starter's gun cracked, it was just Rock and me against a blur of shadowy forms to either side of us. It was a popular race so we were running against the best horses from all over the state.

After the straightaway and most of the way around the first turn, we were boxed in. Momentarily confused, we lost ground until I moved Rock to the outside. Then through the second straightaway we regained ground. Going into the far turn, there were only two horses ahead of us. At that point it was all up to Rock.

Halfway through the last turn he pulled even with the second-place horse. And then as we came out of the turn, his nose was on the rump of the leader. From then on he steadily inched up on him until we were neck and neck. It was a two-horse race for the final hundred yards or so. I could feel Rock straining with every lunge, and hear his breath coming out in loud blasts. The rider next to me frantically whipped his horse.

Rock flashed past the finish pole half a length ahead. The grandstands were strangely silent as I slowed him down. Distantly, I heard the loudspeaker announce the "Indian pony" as the winner.

I was nearly crying until I saw my grandfather, my father, and John walking down the track toward us. They each quietly shook my hand and patted Rock. Then a man led us all to the front of the grandstand. There my grandfather accepted the hundred dollars, and someone threw a red blanket over Rock.

A man in a white hat caught up to us as we made our way back to our wagon and offered to buy Rock. My grandfather said something, and the man in the white hat grabbed me.

"He says it's your horse," he growled. "So I'll make you the offer, son."

I looked at my grandfather, but he just stood with his arms folded across his chest.

"Two hundred dollars," the man went on, thrusting a handful of bills at me.

I shook my head and grabbed Rock's lead rope. We started home.

Two hundred dollars was a lot of money in 1948, and there was a moment later when I regretted not selling Rock.

After this race, we had something of a reputation and felt bound by it to continue racing, which we did. Everyone who imagined he had a fast horse was eager to match up with us. Although we had some close calls, amazingly Rock never lost a race after that day in Fort Pierre.

Everywhere we raced we drew a crowd. Those who had never seen him couldn't believe that Rock was so formidable. He was not tall, a little cow-hocked, always thin, and his overall confirmation was not that of a muscular race horse. But as the summer wore on, he became a hero. People came from remote parts of the reservation to watch him run. Some people even gave him gifts, like an old medicine man who tied a bundle into Rock's mane and warned me never to lose it.

In early September my grandfather decided to rest Rock until the end of the month, after which we would go to the annual fair and celebration at the Reservation Agency.

While Rock rested, we made preparations. My father repaired his old car so he and my mother and grandmother could travel ahead of us. They had our camp set up by the time the rest of us reached the agency, including a small pen for the horses that became a gathering place for young and old. All kinds of people came to see the little paint with flying feet.

At the site of the fair, tents blossomed on the prairie around the dancing arbor and the rodeo grounds. A cloud of dust floated like a shroud over the encampment, raised by the constantly moving people, horses, and automobiles. Smoke from cooking fires rose skyward in thin, white-gray plumes, reminiscent of times long past. Children roamed in groups, while old men sat in circles and talked of old times. Every evening the steady throb of drums drew everyone into the dancing. It was a time of reunion and renewal, a time for invoking the old ways and remembering the glories of the past. And my horse was a connection between then and now.

Horse racing began the second day. There was much betting, and I learned years later that my father wagered his car against fifty dollars cash on our first race. The first day of racing was merely for purposes of elimination. The field of nearly one hundred fifty runners was culled down to ten. Two of them were Rock and the bay.

The final race was the last event of the rodeo on the final day of the fair. As John and I warmed up our horses, I was astonished to see the number of people lining the track. It seemed every Indian on the reservation was there.

As each horse was led to the starting line, its name and the rider's name were announced. Drums pounded, and women trilled. When a judge came to take Rock's reins and pulled us forward, a virtual roar erupted. Although Rock nevertheless took his place calmly, I didn't dare turn my eyes toward the crowds.

To this day I am astounded that Rock meant so much to those people so many years ago. I know now it was because he was a throwback, a connection to a past when life and glory depended on the courage of such a horse. And I knew something else, I felt it. Everyone there wanted Rock to win.

There was utter silence as the starter raised his arm. I had only a simple plan—to let my horse run the three-quarters of a mile any way he wanted. The gun popped, and Rock lunged forward. We stayed in the bunch through the first straightaway and around the first turn. After that it was a race for second place for the rest of the field.

Rock set a deadly pace, and I worried he might burn himself out. But going into the last turn I risked a glance back over my shoulder and gasped out loud. We were ten lengths ahead of the rest of the horses. Coming out of the turn into the final straightaway, Rock increased his lead. Still, he gamely put everything he had into the final sprint. After the race my father said we crossed the finish line some twenty lengths ahead of the field.

That night my grandfather, Rock and I were led into the dancing arbor. Four times we circled behind the singers and drummers as they sang the honor song. Rock bobbed his head in time with the drums. When the song was over, we were given gifts—money, a beaded saddle blanket, quilts, a tent, and more. In turn, my grandfather gave money to the singers and drummers who sang for us. When we finally left the arbor, I noticed that the medicine bundle was gone from Rock's mane.

That night people crowded around our camp to look at Rock. My mother and grandmother boiled pot after pot of coffee until there was no more. It was after midnight when the last visitors left.

My horse was just as curious at the knots of onlookers as they were about him. He stood at the rail and let them scratch his neck and gently rub his nose. It was the old ones, the grand-mothers and grandfathers, who seemed most taken with that skinny paint. Many of them paused to shake my hand, and all I could think of was that day in our corral at home—that day when I wanted my grandfather to get rid of a scraggly paint. Now I couldn't imagine my life without him.

The next morning we broke camp. Like everyone else, we were reluctant to leave. During the three days of the fair amidst the melee of noise and activity we had experienced a feeling of purpose, of belonging, and of strength. But next year it would happen again.

A large group of riders accompanied us as we headed north toward home. They rode with us until they had to turn for home, a rider or two peeling off now and then until there were only our wagon, my parents' car, John on the bay, and Rock and me. Later, my grandmother said it was like the old days with young men and boys on their horses, running and playing, and enjoying life.

Late autumn came, I went back to school, and my father and grandfather finished the harvest. I was glad for the quiet of home and somehow kept finding myself in the gentle presence of my mother and grandmother. The excitement of the summer seemed unreal and far away, and I appreciated their calm strength.

Rock and the bay grazed contentedly most of the time. Once in a while when the urge struck me, I would climb on Rock, and we would fly over the prairies. We galloped for the sheer joy of it, celebrating life and each other, savoring the freedom to go as fast and as far as we chose. Those were the moments I enjoyed most, and remember most often.

As the leaves began to flutter helplessly to the ground and the land was losing its life-affirming green, two white men came to see my grandfather. They wanted one more race, a chance to recover their pride, they said. I hadn't realized that pride was so important. They were willing to bet five hundred dollars against the paint in a head-to-head race against one of their horses. If we won, we would have five hundred dollars. If we lost, we would have to give them Rock.

My grandfather left it up to me. I suppose it was the lure of the money, as much as my confidence in Rock, that pushed me to agree. There were moments much later when I nearly hated the old man for putting the decision in my hands.

The day and the hour of the race were set, and the two white men went away smiling. I wondered what we could buy with five hundred dollars—practically anything, I guessed. Then late one night John came with the news, and I was crushed.

The white men had brought a thoroughbred race horse all the way from the state of Tennessee just to run against my paint. I wanted to withdraw, but my grandfather said we had given our word.

"They are only whites," I argued.

"Maybe," the old man replied, "but it is our word that is important."

We began to prepare Rock, and he seemed to understand that something was in the wind since there was an urgency about the way he pushed himself during the workouts. There was anxiety for the rest of us, too.

Later one night my mother found me crying under my covers. "Part of Rock's strength comes from you believing that he will win," she told me. "He needs that from you."

On the day of the race, we awoke at dawn and started for town as the sun's first red rays streaked the eastern sky. By the time we arrived, the rodeo grounds were already overflowing with people. A small cheer went up as I took Rock out on the track for his warmup.

I began to feel confident until the Tennessee thoroughbred was led out. He was a bright sorrel fully two hands taller than Rock, a bundle of muscles, snorting and dragging his handler around. My body went cold, and I began to sweat.

All too soon we were called to the starting line. A hush fell over the crowd. I could hardly keep my eyes from the snorting sorrel as the judge gave instructions. I could barely concentrate. In a haze I saw the starter's arm go up and nearly lost my balance as Rock lunged forward at the blast of the pistol.

The sorrel immediately bolted ahead of us, but Rock put himself right on the big horse's tail. Yet I felt that it was only a matter of time before the powerful thoroughbred would begin pulling away from us. But he didn't.

Rock shadowed him around the first turn and down the straightaway. I noticed he was running easily, and I began to hope. Then halfway into the far turn I felt him slowing, and I thought it was over. But Rock was slowing because the thoroughbred was slowing. *Rock's strength comes from you believing he will win.* My mother's words seemed to push us, and I began to believe.

Coming out of the turn in the final straightaway, I shifted my weight to the outside and felt Rock ease himself to the right. Slowly, slowly we gained on the pounding sorrel. He looked enormous, and I could see the big horse's muscles pumping furiously as his rider viciously laid the whip to him. At the same time, I could feel Rock lunge harder and harder.

I heard a faint, faraway roar as we began to pull even. Foam from the lathered thoroughbred hit me in the face. His mouth was wide open, reaching desperately for air.

Then it happened. Rock put his head in front and refused to let up. That's how we crossed the finish line.

The crowd poured from the grandstand and mobbed us. People reached out, wanting to touch my horse, pulling at my arms. Somewhere in the crowd an Indian woman trilled for our victory. We had to fight our way back to our wagon.

At the wagon John pulled me off and put a halter on Rock, trying to keep the crowd back. My mother hugged me, while my grandmother gave me a drink of cool water. It was a dream, almost a nightmare.

The sheriff pushed his way through the crowd and put five hundred dollars into my grandfather's hands.

A week later, sometime during the night there was a fire in our old barn, the barn made of hay. The barn was gone in less than twenty minutes. The only horse inside was Rock. He didn't get out in time. Although we managed to keep the fire from spreading, it didn't really matter to me. I had lost my friend.

Once again, word spread quickly. People came from miles around, whites and Indians alike. It was as though a person had died. Men looked sadly at the scorched earth where the barn had stood. Women wept, especially the Indian women. They gave voice to the grief I kept silent.

I helped gather Rock's bones, and we buried him on a particularly lush hillside where he had liked to graze. His grave overlooked the valley, the river, and the prairies where we had played.

Since I've grown to manhood I've returned to the old place several times—once when I went off to war and again when I returned from war. I sat near his grave, remembered, and thanked Rock. I thanked him for all that he had taught me, but especially for teaching me never to give up.

The prairie grasses have mostly reclaimed the old homesite, except for the tiny fenced-in area where my grandparents are buried. My parents visit there often, to remember. They are grandparents now, passing their stories and their wisdom on to my sons and daughters.

The road to the old place is only grassy depressions on the earth. But there is something else—a gentle thunder of pounding hooves, carried by the sighing breezes. My friend is still there. He and my grandparents must be having a good time.

And I have almost forgotten something the old man told me a few years after the fire—something about tire tracks and boot prints in the gully below our place. I guess it was pride, after all.

("Pride" was previously published in *The Reader and Writer Connection: Audience and Purpose,* an anthology published by Artcore and the Casper College Division of Language and Literature, Casper, Wyoming, 1993.)

The Birthday Turtle

▲   Rising from the prairie floor, the pine-covered ridge soon
▲   filled the western horizon as the two men drove toward
▲   it. The shiny new pick-up truck bounced across the
▲   grassy, uneven terrain and hushed to a stop below a shale
▲   outcropping, where the two men stepped down.

The younger man stood tall and straight, the older leaned on a cane.

"Is this where you rode up the ridge, Grandpa?"

The old man shaded his eyes with a gnarled hand, his dark liquid eyes studying the ridge. But he was also looking inside, trying to see backward across seventy-three years.

"Yeah," he replied softly. "Fifteen. I was fifteen that year. It was sunrise. Sun was hitting the east side, shiny, like new coins. The whole ridge was shining like new coins."

The younger man smiled. He knew the words from hearing his grandfather's countless recitations, and he never tired of hearing the story of the turtle, a giant turtle high on the ridge.

"There's that slope." The younger man pointed toward the south end of the ridge. "It's like you said, Grandpa. It's not too steep."

"Yeah. That's where I found the tracks. Old Man Hornsby's cattle walked up that slope. So I rode up after them. I took my

time, 'cause I knew I had all day, and it was going to be hot—
August sixteenth, my birthday. I knew it would be cool up in
them trees. There was a breeze, too."

"Seventy-three years ago."

"Yeah, seventy-three years ago, today."

"Do you think the turtle is still there, Grandpa?"

"Hard to say. If someone went up there since then, maybe
they saw it. Maybe they took it away."

A cool breeze glided down the ridge and caressed their faces.
Above them a lone hawk was already riding the cool air, already
starting his quest for life. Above him the cloudless sky was turning brighter as the sun rose higher, though night's dark hues still
clung grimly to the far western horizon. The clear, sharp notes of
a meadowlark's song floated across the prairie. The old man
smiled.

"Do you know what he said?"

Jon Marichale looked at his grandfather. Under his battered
straw hat, Abel Two Heart's hair was mostly gray and on his face
was carved all eighty-eight years of his life.

"No, Grandpa."

"He said *Nitinkta ca yagli hwo.* Have you come home to die?"

"Who told you that, Grandpa?"

"My grandmother, your great-great grandmother."

Abel looked around at the open land stretching out in every
direction. His nostrils flared as he drew in the cool morning air,
filling his lungs.

"When your mother was a little girl we lived over there," he
pointed south, "just above Soldier Creek. Lightning struck Little
Butte, made the earth slide, uncover a shiny, white stone, big as
your truck. Round. We saw it. The relatives and neighbors came
and looked at it. Henry Ames was the Agency boss farmer that
time. The last one. He came 'cause he heard about the rock. I
think he talked to some other whites. They came, dug out the
stone, and took it away in a big truck. No one knows where they
took it."

The old man waved toward the ridge. "So, maybe someone saw the turtle, like I did. If it was a white person, then they prob'-ly took it away. Like they did that big rock."

"So you think the turtle's gone?"

The old man shrugged his thin shoulders. "Don't know. We should go look."

Worry flickered across the younger man's face. "It's a long climb, Grandpa. It's going to get hot, too."

"I live a long time, Grandson. One more climb will be good. One more hill to add, one more hill to remember. You live long enough, you climb a lot of hills."

Jon opened the door to the truck and grabbed a large back-pack with a trenching tool tied to it, and two canteens of water. They had been planning this for days—a walk up Turtle Butte, as Abel Two Heart called the ridge. On the topographic maps it had no name, it was just a sudden high ridge on an otherwise gently rolling, mostly flat prairie.

The ridge meant nothing to anyone else. It was just there. But it held a memory for the old man. A memory made when he was still a boy, almost a young man.

Jon put on the backpack, crammed mostly with food pre-pared by his wife, his mother, and his grandmother. It was heavy. The canteens he strapped around his waist. As an afterthought he put on a baseball cap. Finally, from the bed of the truck he took a bow and quiver of arrows.

The old man smiled at the sight of the bow and arrows. He pointed at the primitive Lakota bow. "Best one I ever made," he said.

"I know. It's brought down eight deer. Last year the curator from the museum at the university wanted to buy it." Jon point-ed to the slope. "Are you ready, Grandpa?"

"Yeah. It's a good day. What do you suppose the women cooked for us?"

"Whatever it is, it's heavy."

They started up the slope, Jon leaning under his pack. They

had walked the prairies together over the years and climbed more than a few hills. As a boy Jon had followed his grandfather everywhere, eagerly and unquestioningly. Often he would walk in the same footsteps as the old man. At first his small footprints were visible within his grandfather's larger ones. But as the years went by and he grew, they eventually left one trail, as if only one man had passed.

Abel Two Heart remembered these things as he walked steadily behind his grandson. He was the follower now, trusting in his grandson's ability to find the right path.

At a certain point they paused and looked out over the prairie. They were up high already and it looked as if the prairie had grown, the horizons stretching out.

The old man leaned on his cane and pointed to the southwest. "Blackpipe," he said, "over there. My stepfather was from there. The BIA put up corrals and a house for the boss farmer. We went there to get our issues—rice, beans, salt, and meat. The men would kill the longhorn cows and drag them to the creek. Then the women would butcher."

"When did he die, your stepfather, I mean?"

"Twenty-one. Nineteen twenty-one. A year before I married your grandmother."

"He could make medicine?"

"Yeah. He knew plants. He could cure toothaches, make a poultice that could stop bleeding, make a tea that would fix bad stomach troubles."

"And your father died in eighteen ninety-six?"

"Yeah. He was about thirty-eight or thirty-nine, I think. He was about seventeen or eighteen when he was at the Greasy Grass Fight, what the whites call the Battle of the Little Bighorn. Spanish flu, they called it—the sickness that took him. When he knew he was dying, he finally told us about the Greasy Grass Fight."

"Finally?"

"Yeah. Some people told him, warned him not to tell anyone

that he fought. Some were afraid that the whites would take him away because he was there when their big chief Custer was killed."

"So you didn't know until you were eight, that Great-grand-pa Justin was in the Greasy Grass Fight?"

"That's right. My mother knew, but she never asked him."

Jon looked up at the hawk who was still prowling the skies. Far off to the east a thin line of dust rose into the air as a vehicle traveled a gravel road. His own truck looked small on the prairie floor.

"I remember you saying that he wanted a meal?"

"Yeah. He asked my mother to cook us all a good meal, he had something to tell us. So she did and we ate. We had a willow shade in the back of the house, that time. He liked to lay there in the open, feel the wind on his face and look out at the land. We ate and he told us the story of what he did in the Greasy Grass Fight. All afternoon and into the evening, he talked."

The old man paused to tap the ground in a rhythm like the beating of a heart. A few soft phrases from an ancient song escaped his lips. The younger man joined in, murmuring his song softly. It was an old ritual, an honoring song sung for a warrior who had died young. It was a ritual performed each time the old man's father was mentioned in any way.

The song floated away on the breeze and the old man stared out across the prairies, as if watching it go.

"He told everything," he went on. "The big encampment along the Greasy Grass River, the horses. More than he could count, he said. The fighting. I listened, he was a good storyteller, and I could hear the guns booming and cracking, horses running, the dust hanging in the air. Screams and yells, soldiers going down. One every few heartbeats, he said."

"He was so young," said Jon.

"In years, but he was a man that day. He said he left his boyhood there."

Jon readjusted the pack and glanced up the slope. "What do you think, Grandpa? Shall we go?"

The old man's eyes twinkled. "If you feel rested."

They climbed slowly as the sun rose higher, following an old cutback trail. Near the summit they stopped again, and the prairie had grown larger again. It was immense. After a few moments the old man pointed to a low, hogback ridge about a mile off.

"Good place for pipestone," he said. "Makes the black pipes. That's where the Blackpipe settlement got its name. It was during the Ghost Dance doings, back in 1889, I think. Some of them did the Ghost Dance here 'cause no whites lived around here then. No one to see them and turn them in to the government. Anyway, that hill still has good pipe stone. Shale, I think it's called."

"And it turns black after you bake it in the ground with a fire over it?"

"Yeah. Then you rub it with grease of some kind, it turns shiny."

"Maybe we'll stop there on the way home and do some digging. I haven't made a pipe for a couple of years."

The old man nodded. "Yeah. The world can always use another good pipe. Good pipe, good smoke, good prayers. The spirits would like that, so would our relatives."

They were not far from the summit and the edge of the small pine and cedar forest that blanketed the ridge top. Already they could hear the breeze singing softly in the cedar branches. Jon Marichale glanced at his grandfather and was relieved to see no signs of strain on the old man's face. The climb up was not steep, but it was steady. Then he remembered that the old man had a CCC job in the 1930s where all he did was walk.

"Grandpa," he said, as he readjusted his pack again. "How long did you have that CCC job, where you helped build that dam?"

The old man nodded, diving into his memories again.

"From May until October that year," he replied. "1934."

"You walked from home, and back?"

"Every day, except Sunday. Six miles to the dam, then all day behind a team of four horses pulling a big scoop, and then six miles home. I would start walking at four o'clock in the morning, get there at six-thirty, get my horses and hitch them up. We got a meal break at twelve, until one. Quit at six, put up the scoop and see to the horses, and then I would get home after eight. Your grandma would have supper ready for me so I would eat and go to bed. Start all over the next day."

"Damn, Grandpa, I don't think I could do that."

"You could if you had to. I did it 'cause I had to, not because I wanted to. Your grandma didn't have it easy either, that time. Your uncle was four and your mom was six. She had to take care of them, plant a garden and take care of it. Take care of our six cows, chickens. It was a hard time for everybody."

Jon looked back down the slope. "I didn't see any cattle tracks."

"No. There's nothing in the pastures now. I don't know whose land this is now, prob'ly some white rancher. It was still Indian land when I came here looking for Hornsby's cows in 1903. In 1910 they opened up the reservation to whites, the Homestead Act. Now they own most of the reservation."

"Uncle Matthew was telling me the other day he came across some old records in the BIA land office, from the 1920s, I think he said. Some whites bought Indian land for thirty cents an acre, I guess."

"Yeah. They lease it for a few dollars an acre now. You should hear Herman Kerrigan cry around every spring when he comes to pay lease to your grandma. Says four dollars an acre is way too much. Can't make money, he says. I'm glad all whites aren't like him. Sad thing is most of 'em are."

They both looked toward the trees. The ridge top wasn't exactly flat and it was only about fifty yards wide, but it felt like its own world.

"Did people come up here a lot, when you were a boy, Grandpa?"

"Indians did, I know that. On the north end is a rise that some used for *hanbleceya*, the vision quest. I don't know about now." The old man looked around, studying the ground. "No people tracks."

Without another word they turned toward the trees, walking in silence. The air among the trees was still cool and the song of the breeze through the cedars was soothing, inviting. Birds fluttered about or glided in among the trees—magpies, a few chickadees, and a flicker. Somewhere ahead of them a red-headed woodpecker drummed slowly.

There was no path or trail as such among the trees on the ridge top, only openings between the pines and cedars, and the occasional sumac.

"I rode to the north end," recalled the old man. "The trees were not as thick then, maybe. On my way back I saw the gully that opened out to the east. I could see a long way out across the prairie, so I tied up the horse and walked toward the end of it. That's where I saw the turtle, in the gully."

They walked a few more yards and the old man pointed to the right. "There," he said, "that's the gully. I know it."

The gully started in the middle of the ridge top and sloped down until it ended abruptly. At the top it was shallow and narrow, at the head it was deep and a few yards wide, a window looking out over the prairie.

They followed the cut, meandering between the exposed roots of trees. Near the end its walls were nearly vertical and higher than the younger man was tall. But they saw nothing that resembled a giant turtle.

"A good view," said the old man, gazing out across the miles of prairie. "Just like I remembered it."

"Where was the turtle?"

Abel gestured backward. "There. 'Bout halfway."

"And one foot was sticking out from the back, and it was

head down with its back to the east."

The old man nodded. "Yeah." He held up a hand, palm down, about thigh high. "This far up the bank. I thought it was nothing but a flat rock and I tried to knock it loose from the bank. But it was solid, so I kept digging at it. I dug and dug until I uncovered half of it. The shell was three feet long and it prob'ly would have been two feet high."

Jon Marichale unloaded his pack and canteens. "Does the gully look the same or is it wider, do you think?"

Abel looked hard, trying to match the moment with seventy-three-year-old memories. "Hard to say," he concluded. "But things change. Lot of snow and rain has come down in seventy-three years. Widened the gully, made it deeper. Carried off my turtle, maybe."

"Or maybe it slid down to the gully floor and has been covered over."

"Yeah, that could happen, too."

"What do you think, Grandpa? What shall we do?"

"Grandson, we came up here to look for a turtle. Let's look."

"Okay."

"But first let's have some coffee."

The younger man chuckled as he opened his backpack.

They made a camp halfway down the gully, about where the old man remembered the turtle was. From the backpack Jon pulled out roast beef sandwiches, *wasna* (pemmican), skillet bread, a container of baked beans, another of fried potatoes, two thermos jugs of coffee, and plates and utensils.

"I guess they thought we were going away for a week or two," the old man said.

"Well, you know how Mom and Grandma are."

"My granddaughter, your wife, is just like them."

"We better eat it all, if we know what's good for us."

The old man smiled as he poured coffee.

"Grandpa, did you tell anyone about the turtle, other than Grandma, I mean?"

The old man shook his head. "No. Nobody but your grandma and me knew what I saw. Before I left I covered it and packed the dirt down. I figured if I saw it, someone else could, too. So I tried to hide it as good as I could. I wanted to bring it down at first. Then I thought: Who am I to disturb that turtle's final resting place?"

"And you never came back?"

"No. I worked for Hornsby one summer and I did come several times to dig pipestone from that hill over to the east. But I never came back up here."

"You think someone did find it and took it down?"

"Could happen, I guess. If anyone did, no one heard about it. That turtle would have been big news. You know how whites like that sort of thing. Big turtle, big news. Could make someone famous, maybe some big money. Who knows? Something else I thought of over the years. How did that turtle get up here and why was it so big?"

Jon Marichale leaned back with his cup of coffee. "I checked into that once," he told the old man. "Seems this whole area might have been an inland sea thousands of years ago, maybe millions. If that's true, then your turtle is a sea turtle."

"A sea turtle? Are they big?"

"Huge."

"How did it turn into stone?"

"A process called petrifaction, where something turns to stone. It takes a long time, thousands of years, maybe hundreds of thousands."

The old man was intrigued. "How does it happen?"

"Well, when something dies and it happens to be in a place where conditions are right, as the organic material decays the space it leaves is filled in by sand or limestone, something harder than the organic stuff. Over time it becomes harder and harder, it becomes stone."

"So what I saw was not really a turtle?"

"Right."

The old man mulled over the information as he sipped on coffee. "That turtle was here a long time, then. I saw it seventy-three years ago, a long time for me, nothing for the turtle. Makes me feel so small, like a flea. Only the Earth lives forever, they say."

"Wait a minute, I brought something." Jon reached into his shirt pocket and pulled out a folded paper. "Look at this," he said, unfolding it. "Is this what your turtle looked like?"

The old man looked at the picture of a sea turtle. Its head and shell were like the snapping turtles found in the lakes, rivers, and ponds on the Plains. But its feet were more like fins, or paddles. His eyes grew wide.

"Yeah, this is my turtle."

"We have to find it, then."

"Yeah. But we finish our coffee first."

They started digging at a point halfway down the gully, where the turtle had been seventy-three years ago. By noon they had worked their way down and back up the gully from the point, about twenty feet in both directions, digging at three-foot intervals. Downslope they had stopped at a point even with a long dead cedar on the edge of the gully, its tall gray trunk a stark contrast to the full, green branches all around. They didn't find the turtle. Around noon they took a break to eat.

Overhead the distant, muted roar of a jetliner could be heard briefly over the singing of the breeze in the cedar branches. Between the treetops they could see a long, thin trail of white.

"Tell me," the old man said, pausing in between bites, as he gestured upward. "How is it to ride in one of those things? Must be noisy, huh?"

The old man had never flown in an airplane, though he had confessed to riding in a train once.

"No, it isn't. You can hear the engine, but inside the cabin it isn't noisy. Except when everyone talks at once."

"They let you talk?"

Jon Marichale smiled. "They pass out food on the longer flights."

"They have toilets?"

"Yeah."

"That's a good thing."

"You're right, believe me."

"Is it scary? Were you afraid?"

"Sometimes, when I think about it. But more people get killed in car accidents every year than in plane crashes."

The old man stared up at the condensation trail left by the airliner. "It leaves a trail," he commented. "Still, it's long ways up. A long, long way to fall. Tell me, Grandson, do you really think they went to the moon?"

"I think so."

"You know, that's good."

"How so, Grandpa?"

"One day maybe all the whites will pack up and fly to the moon and stay there, and we can have the land back. Good thing to wish for, huh?"

"I never thought of it that way, but—yeah, that is a good thing to wish for."

"The bad part is they would find a way to spoil it, the moon, I mean. That would be bad for the moon."

"Yeah, it would be."

They ate in silence for a time, listening to the soothing song of the breeze in the cedars. From below faintly came the song of the meadowlark: *Nitinkta ca yagli hwo*—have you come home to die?

A loud CRACK suddenly broke the silence. The dead, gray cedar had finally given way to the crush of years and the relentlessness of decay. Most of its trunk fell into the gully and rolled, coming to a stop against the opposite bank.

The two men looked at one another, even the old man was surprised.

"When I was a boy I saw lightning strike a tree. Ash, it was. I told my stepfather and he asked me to show him where it was. He said such a tree made the best kind of bow, because it had taken on the power of the lightning and the thunders." He pointed toward the gray trunk now lying in the gully. "This I have never seen happen. A tree knocked over by time. We should take a small piece of it with us, to remind us that everything is born and everything dies. No matter if it has roots, or wings, or legs, or if it crawls on its belly. It is the thing that makes us all the same. All of us."

"We'll take a piece with us, Grandpa."

They finished their meal. Even in the shade of the pines they could feel the heat of the August day. The old man strolled to the end of the gully and gazed again out over the land. The younger man followed. Below and to their right they could see the truck, shiny in the afternoon sun.

"Grandson," Abel said, "I would like to see an arrow fly from here, into the sky and down to the Earth. That is if my old eyes can see it."

Smiling, Jon went after his bow, strung it and nocked an arrow, drew back, and aimed it toward the east. "Get ready, Grandpa."

With a twang the bow launched the arrow. It flashed upward into the sunlight and then arched downward and disappeared into the late summer hues below the horizon.

"Did you see it, Grandpa?"

"Yeah! Before it went down! It was a fine thing, a fine thing! It is like life. We fly high and far, if we can, and then we go home, back to the Earth."

Jon nocked and loosed a second arrow and they watched it fly, almost in the same rainbow path as the first.

The old man gazed long at the far horizon, long after the arrow had landed. There was something in those old eyes that Jon had never seen before. A look, a mixture of sadness and joy, and perhaps anticipation.

Abel touched his grandson's shoulder. "Thank you for that, Grandson. I have one other favor to ask."

"Anything you want, Grandpa."

"When I die you must loose an arrow toward the sun so that my spirit can ride on it into the other world."

Jon Marichale's eyes misted a little. "I'll do that, Grandpa. I'll do that."

They stood shoulder to shoulder gazing toward the far horizon, losing track of time, as they had many times in the past. The hawk was still in the sky, hanging on the winds, gliding effortlessly. Suddenly she rose higher and higher until they lost sight of her.

"Grandpa, what about the turtle?"

"Oh, I think it is lost. We will not find it today."

They turned and walked back up the gully, settling back down at their camp. Along the way Jon had picked up a piece from the dead and fallen cedar.

"I'm sorry we couldn't find your turtle, Grandpa. Maybe someone found it."

"Maybe, but I feel that it is still here. The heavy rains or the melting snows could have moved it, and buried it. Perhaps they buried it deeper than we can dig."

"I wish you could have seen it again."

"Yeah, me too. But maybe you will, or perhaps one of your children will. What is three human lifetimes to a thing that has spent eternity here?"

The afternoon sun was close to the western horizon by the time they packed their things and started back down the slope. In the east the night was beginning to push its shadow up over the horizon, a thin line of darkness rimming the distant hills and prairies.

"This was a good day," the old man said. "I find it hard to believe that I have been on this Earth for eighty-eight years."

"I think Mom and Grandma invited some people over tonight," Jon said.

"It will be good to see relatives. Well, most of them, anyway."

"There'll be gifts, Grandpa. Darlene and I and the kids got you something. Something special."

"I know it will be as good as what the turtle gave me today," the old man said.

He paused at the top of the south slope, looking around again.

"What do you mean, Grandpa? What did the turtle give you?"

"This day," the old man replied without hesitation. "This day with my grandson."

Jon Marichale nodded, not trusting to speak over the lump in his throat.

Halfway down the slope a meadowlark floated by, singing its song. *Nitinkta ca yagli hwo*—have you come home to die?

The old man smiled and nodded, and followed his grandson down the slope.

It was a good day. A day Jon Marichale would never forget.

At his grandfather's funeral, as the singers sang the honoring song to the soft pounding of a drum beating like a heart, he sent an arrow into the sun.

The Bloodlines of Heritage

▲ Labels too frequently hide the essence of what they iden-
▲ tify. They are the surface of reality and never reveal the
▲ depth. When a label is applied, it is too often out of neg-
▲ ativity or derision, and certainly ignorance.
▲   Many labels have been applied to the indigenous
peoples of this continent. Some are innocent and
innocuous, and some are harmful; but most are mis-
leading. In addition to labels given by people of other
races, indigenous groups of the past also labeled one
another, usually depending on whether they were friends
or foes. For example, the Ojibway labeled my ancestors
naddewasioux, meaning "little snakes" or "little enemies,"
for obvious reasons. The Pawnee called the Nanahe
Arapaho, meaning "traders." A recent label which
emerged from the early Indian activist period of the
1960s was *apple*—someone red on the outside but white
on the inside, in other words, an Indian person guided
by white values.
Europeans labeled us when they came to this land, and Euro-
Americans continue to do so. Their labels were and are based predominantly on fear, misunderstanding, condescension, and bigotry. *Savage, child of nature, pagan, heathen, godless, chief, princess,
welfare tribe,* and *prairie nigger* are some of the more memorable
ones. Some labels are not as obviously biased or bigoted but can

still cause confusion.

Historians, anthropologists, and other researchers and scholars have committed their share of faux pas when writing or talking about indigenous peoples. For example, when the seven Lakota groups are listed or discussed, their names are given in a mixture of Lakota, English, and French—something like the following:

Oglala—they scatter their own,

Two Kettle—two boilings,

Hunkpapa—people who camp on the end,

Sans Arc—without bows,

Blackfeet—(not the Blackfeet of Montana),

Brule—burnt leg or burnt thing, and

Mniconju—those who plant by the water.

In this instance, the names in order of usage are Lakota, English, Lakota, French, English, French, and Lakota.

To me, it would be more logical to list those seven names *all in Lakota, all in English,* or *all in French.* As one who is fairly fluent in Lakota, I would prefer to have the names listed in Lakota—but perhaps that approach would be too logical.

Still, ironically such a linguistic mishmash of labels does serve a purpose—it shows that labels have staying power and, like bad habits, can be hard to change. For example, I (like most Indians) often answer questions regarding my particular tribal affiliation, and the conversation usually goes something like this:

Them: What is your tribe, by the way?

Me: Sicangu Lakota.

Them: Really? I don't think I've heard of them.

Me: Have you heard of Rosebud Sioux?

Them: Yes, I think so. Is that the same as Brule?

Me: It's the same group.

Them: Of course, then you're Brule?

Me: I prefer Sicangu Lakota.

Them: How nice. But the world thinks of you as Brule.

Me: Whatever.

Lost in such eclectic misnomers and hidden by all the long-held labels is the issue of *heritage*. To examine this issue, we must consider and confront some labels—labels that are intra-cultural, centuries old, and not necessarily exclusive to one indigenous tribe or another. These labels are *full-blood* and *mixed-blood*. They originated as early as the 1600s when Europeans intermarried among the indigenous groups, producing offspring of mixed racial and cultural backgrounds.

The motivation for such intermarriage was predominantly entrepreneurial. Furs were plentiful in what the Europeans called the "New World," but there was one major obstacle to supplying buyers in Europe—procurement. It was an obstacle because European fur traders in North America by and large did not know the land. The natives obviously did, and while furs harvested by natives were acquired in trade by Europeans, as true entrepreneurs they soon realized that by eliminating the middle man—the native hunter and trapper—the cost of procurement could be lowered.

More than likely it was the French who came up with the idea of commingling with the natives in order to gain firsthand knowledge of the land, as well as the skills to hunt and trap fur-bearing animals. The initial step was probably simply to live among the indigenous peoples, thereby acquiring the requisite knowledge and skills. Soon, however, Frenchmen began to take native wives. Whether such individuals were driven purely by business motives, male desires, or felt genuine emotion for their wives is an interesting question, perhaps worthy of scholarly research. Whatever their motivations, children born of such unions were half native and half white, and immediately burdened with the negative connotations of their mixed racial heritage—a burden that neither society has lifted entirely.

From the beginning, the "cup is half empty" kind of thinking was prevalent regarding children of mixed parentage. Each race felt that the child of such a union was diminished by the

other race. In some instances, such a child was not even regarded as a whole person. Hence the labels of *breed* and *half-breed*
quickly emerged. Originating in Canada, *métis* was the term
applied specifically to children of native and French parentage.

If such labels did not originate as negative appellations,
many quickly became that. A sad consequence was mistreatment
of children with mixed racial heritage, ranging from verbal to
physical abuse. Today, such mistreatment is not as prevalent, and
one hopes that it is on a steady decline. However, centuries-old
negative perceptions still exist.

Those who perceive themselves to be *full-blood* regard those
who are *mixed-blood* as inferior, perhaps even dispossessed of
heritage. Those who are mixed-blood are certainly aware of the
perception held by full-bloods, and there is a retaliatory tendency to think of full-bloods as backwards, perhaps unable or
unwilling to fully participate in modern society.

Mixed-bloods far outnumber full-bloods, with some estimates placing the latter at 10 percent of the overall Indian population. This factor only serves to intensify negative feelings and
exacerbate differences.

Also part of the debate is the possibility that at some point
in the future there might be no more full-blood Indians. But
does that mean that descendants of the various indigenous peoples of this continent will cease to exist as viable representatives
of their cultures? The answer to that question can be found in
any Indian group or community today. Even if it is probable that
only 10 percent of all Indians are full-bloods, and if the strength
of Indian cultures was solely attributable to the number of full-
bloods, then Indian cultures should be virtually nonexistent
today. However, the fact remains that Indian cultures are
stronger today than they have been in many years.

If a decrease in the average degree of native or Indian blood
does not result in a commensurate loss of culture, what is the
reason? The only obvious answer is heritage. Heritage, however,
cannot be entirely separated from bloodline because it is some-

thing that comes through birth. To inherit is to take or receive by succession from predecessors.

My siblings and I were born of mixed parentage in terms of bloodline. Our mother is a full-blood Sicangu Lakota, and our father is a mix of predominantly Oglala and some French. Considering that French surnames are in abundance on the rolls of just about every reservation in South Dakota, our family situation is not at all unusual. But of the eleven children in my family, I am the only one whose primary language is Lakota.

My siblings and I all have the same degree of Indian blood. We are enrolled as eleven-sixteenths Rosebud Sioux, or Sicangu Lakota. Due to the nature of enrollment requirements, which vary slightly from tribe to tribe, our Oglala blood is not recognized. Overall, however, we are seven-eighths Lakota and one-eighth French.

Enrollment is, of course, a legal requirement for tribal membership since the establishment of federal reservations. Though minimum blood quantum (or quantity of blood) is often established by tribal councils, enrollment records are kept by Bureau of Indian Affairs agencies (BIA administrative offices located on reservations). Minimum blood quantum for enrollment in most Sioux (Lakota, Dakota, and Nakota) tribes is one-fourth. Therefore, if you can prove at least one-fourth Rosebud Sioux blood, for example—though you may be three-fourths anything else, including non-Indian—you can be legally enrolled as a member of the Rosebud Sioux Tribe.

Legal requirement for tribal enrollment is based primarily on genealogy, with the enablement of biology—in other words, knowing one's ancestry due to birth. Meeting the legal requirement for tribal enrollment simply means one has proven bloodlines. This is the beginning of heritage; that is, one inherits certain *physical* (hence racial and biological) characteristics of skin and hair color, body type, family resemblances, and so on. The other aspect of heritage is *ethnicity*, which is abstract and therefore less perceptible. Does physical heritage guarantee ethnic heritage? I think not.

To completely inherit the essence of what one is racially and ethnically, one must learn the stories of family, community, and tribe (or nation) in order to learn the culture. To learn one's inherited culture, means to learn and eventually use language, traditions, values, and customs.

It is entirely possible, therefore, to be physically and biologically Indian and never learn the ethnic and cultural aspects of one's tribal heritage. Consider the following story.

Sometime in the early 1800s a group of Crow warriors raided a small Lakota village just northeast of the Black Hills. Captives were taken, among them a boy less than four years old. Upon returning to their own territory and village, the Crow warriors gave the boy to a family who had lost a child.

That Crow family raised the boy as their own. The passage of time and the solicitous attentions of his adoptive parents erased the boy's memories of his Lakota childhood. His first language faded as he learned to think and converse in Crow. In time, the stories of his adopted family, band, and tribe overshadowed his biological roots, and his heritage became Crow.

As a young man, the former Lakota boy participated in raids against his biological relatives. His loyalties, motives, and interests were completely Crow, and he was not hesitant to take up arms against the Lakota.

Eventually, the young man courted and won the love of a young woman, married, and raised a family. He and his wife taught their children Crow values, traditions, customs, and history. Not once did he mention that he was biologically a Lakota because that part of him had been totally erased. Though his *bloodline* would always be Lakota, his *heritage* became and remained Crow. As far as the particular family and band which adopted that boy was concerned, the boy was Crow. The entire community had helped raise him as a Crow, contributing to and enhancing his heritage, knowing that what they were giving him would be much stronger than blood.

Blood does not guarantee heritage. Heritage must be acquired. Most people born into a family and community gradually learn about their heritage from members of their birth family and community. Although the Lakota child who became a Crow in every sense of the word except for blood is an exception, examples such as this should serve to remind us that bloodline and heritage are separate.

I recently met a young man in France who was Omaha but had grown up in Europe, raised by an adoptive Belgian mother. Although physically he was obviously native to North America, his cultural ties had been weakened because he had been raised in another country. Although his adoptive family had not intentionally prevented him from knowing his native heritage, and in fact had encouraged him to learn about it, circumstances simply had not allowed him to fully embrace the culture connected with his bloodline.

Heritage is the reason that several indigenous cultures have survived to this point in the twentieth century, and will continue to survive. Certainly, bloodlines or blood quantums have been diluted, and aspects of many indigenous cultures have been lost. But that loss has less to do with the decrease in blood degree and more to do with the attitudes, policies, and actions of Europeans and Euro-Americans. Hand in hand with several Christian denominations, the federal government has unabashedly stated and implemented its intention to "kill the Indian and save the man," a slogan which was the cornerstone of assimilation policy.

Assimilation was an approach taken in the earliest days of white colonialism. Believing that they were bestowing a better life on indigenous peoples, the proponents of assimilation worked to Christianize and "civilize" Indians. Their true motive, of course, was the removal of Indians from lands desired by whites. Consequences were the suppression of indigenous cultures and the adoption of white traditions and values by indigenous peoples—all of which served to adversely affect and otherwise interrupt the normal passage of heritage from one generation of indigenous peoples to the next—but not completely.

In order for anyone to pass on one's racial and ethnic heritage, one must understand it and live according to its values, traditions, and customs. In other words, one must practice one's heritage, even under the most difficult circumstances.

Consider the Cheyenne captives who were held at Fort Marion, Florida, in the 1860s. Their ledger drawings are considered examples of the human spirit's ability to transcend adversity. More to the point, these drawings are examples of not only the emotional and spiritual strength of those Cheyenne who endured imprisonment but the strength of spirit demonstrated by indigenous peoples of this continent.

Moreover, these ledger drawings, which are a consequence of a difficult time for those individual Cheyennes, afford us a glimpse of not only hardships endured but of the heritage of those artists. Many of the drawings were of individual exploits and experiences which occurred prior to imprisonment—expressions of a yearning for and a remembrance of better times. These drawings do not provide a single clue regarding the blood quantum of their creators because that was not important to them. Rather, the drawings emanated from and expressed the heritage which had given the artists their essences as Cheyenne people— a heritage that sustained them during an extremely difficult interlude.

Today, there are many native artists in Canada and the United States expressing themselves in various mediums and styles. To look at a work of art, or hear the drum or flute played, is to see, touch, and hear an expression of heritage, and not a verification of blood degree. But in other areas of Indian life the issue of blood degree is still a factor.

To the larger non-Indian society, an Indian is an Indian is an Indian, by and large. Sincere curiosity does not seem to delineate between full-bloods and mixed-bloods; neither does racism and bigotry. Like the overwhelming majority of Indians in the United States and Canada—if not all—I have experienced both racism and bigotry, and strangely the pain of it was not reduced in proportion to the quantity of my white blood. I can't say I only felt eleven-sixteenths or seven-eighths of the sting. And I'm sure someone who is half Indian will never say they felt only half the insult from a racial epithet or a condescending glare.

The labels stemming from degree of Indian blood continue to be a sensitive issue within the Indian community. On some western reservations, the issue moves to center stage when election time rolls around, especially in regards to the offices of tribal president or chairman and vice president or vice chairman.

The full-blood factions want a leader who is more *traditional*, one who speaks the native language and knows the old values. Mixed-blood factions, on the other hand, think that someone who is *progressive* will make a better leader for the times, one who is aware of the current state of affairs. Full-bloods want a leader who will not forget them; mixed-bloods want a leader who is not stuck in the past. The irony is that both sides have entirely viable concerns, yet they apparently fail to see that the real issue is not *bloodline* or *degree of Indian blood*. The real issue is *heritage*.

Purity of bloodline, generally speaking, was probably never attainable among the indigenous tribes of this continent. To be sure, there were those who attempted to maintain it. However, the simple practice of bringing captives into a family, band, and community diluted the host bloodline. Like the Lakota boy raised to be Crow, some of those captives were children who grew up to marry and become parents. Others were adolescent or adult women who became wives and then mothers. In each case, a different tribal bloodline was introduced into the family, band, and community. But, in each case, though the *bloodline* was diluted, *heritage* was not.

Historically, if purity of bloodline was a critical issue and maintaining it was a strictly regimented practice, why did many tribes bring captives from different tribes into their tribes, and why did the tribes of the eastern seaboard allow European men to take their daughters as wives and produce racially mixed children?

The answer to both of the foregoing questions, I believe, is that the indigenous peoples of this continent considered heritage to be stronger than blood. Not that bloodline was considered inconsequential to any extent, because it was not. Rather, I believe that the essence of being Passamaquoddy, or being Seminole, Choctaw, Wampanoag, Hopi, Lakota, and so on, comes from the intangible, the less obvious.

The latest counts have placed the indigenous population in the United States at just over two million. Statistics indicate that 40 percent of us live on reservations and 60 percent off reservations. About 140 native languages are still spoken among the nearly 400 ethnically identifiable tribes still in existence. It is more difficult to assess the percentage of native speakers among the tribes who maintain their languages, but it is probably highest among the Yupik, Inuit, Pima, Navajo, and Lakota (though not necessarily in that order).

There are at least two compelling reasons why, in spite of many losses, indigenous cultures are still alive on Earth Island, or Turtle Island, otherwise known as North America. First, there are still racially and ethnically identifiable descendants of the first inhabitants of this continent—that is, there is still indigenous blood. And second, cultural heritage has been passed down from one generation to the next despite the dilution of indigenous blood. There are nearly thirty Indian colleges in this country on Indian reservations. The primary reason for their establishment and existence is the preservation of indigenous culture and heritage. One example is Haskell Indian University, which changed its name from Haskell Indian Junior College and seems to have altered its mission from being a primary instrument of assimilation to being an institution focused on preserving indigenous culture and heritage.

It is my firm belief that sometime in the future, when the non-Indian society in this country has lost its best values and cultural traditions, as well as its connection to the natural environment, the indigenous cultures will stand ready to rescue it.

And those indigenous cultures can and will do so because we have not lost our heritage.

No matter what we are labeled—American Indians, First Nations, Native Americans, Indigenous Peoples—we are strong. But our strength does not come from numbers; it comes from our tenacious hold on heritage. Though others may perceive us collectively or generically, and label us accordingly, we think of ourselves in connection with our individual tribal identities. Collectively we are strong because we have individually held onto the tradition of passing down heritage from one generation to the next. Our spiritual beliefs and moral codes have been consistent because of that heritage, and overall have not changed under the pressure of populism.

It is relatively simple for anyone to see the tangible aspects of Indian heritage. Pow-wows are more popular than ever as a spectator sport, and non-Indians flock to see the pageantry of drumbeat, dances, and colorful costumes. What is not so obvious is the blood degree of the Indians who dance, and it's just as well. The degree of Indian or indigenous blood is important because it is the beginning of heritage. But it is language, social values, spiritual beliefs, and plain old tradition handed down from the previous generation which complete the identity of being Navajo, Duwamish, Osage, Mohican, or any other tribe.

Interestingly, there has been considerable intermarriage among Indian tribes in this century—much more so than before. I have nieces and nephews who are Lakota and Navajo. In such instances, it is usually the heritage of the mother which is passed down, though not to the exclusion of the father's culture. So while a Lakota/Navajo whose mother is Navajo may grow up to be more aware of his or her Navajo heritage, the most important part of the process is that heritage is passed down.

My maternal grandparents, who raised me, were my connection to Lakota heritage. Because of them I grew up speaking and thinking Lakota, and the stories and lessons I heard were all in Lakota. My French blood comes from my paternal grandfather,

Charles Marshall. I cannot recall any of my relatives ever denouncing or ridiculing that part of my identity. However, there were moments when cautionary remarks were made about the *iyeska*, which is the Lakota expression for mixed-blood and is literally translated as "speaks white." Such remarks, though, were not a universal condemnation of all mixed-bloods but a warning to be careful of those mixed-bloods who had no awareness of Lakota heritage.

My mother's identity and heritage are unquestionable. The physical characteristics she inherited biologically complement her essence, her heritage, as a Lakota woman—all of which were given to her by my maternal grandparents. My father's situation is slightly different. Because of his sandy hair and blue eyes, inherited from his French grandfather Joseph Marshall (or Marichal), Indians and non-Indians alike have often assumed that he is not Indian. Ambivalence over his ancestry dissolves to some extent when he speaks Lakota, which he does fluently. But for me the values by which he has lived speak the loudest, because the Lakota heritage he received from his parents and grandmother more than compensates for the lack of a purer Lakota bloodline.

Finally, while an individual can be Indian by blood alone, there is much more to being Indian than biology. To be Indian is to know one's culture, to speak one's native language if possible, to live by ancient values and spiritual beliefs, and to be aware of the hardships of the past five hundred years and to have experienced it in one's own life. To be Indian is to be aware of the trail we have walked as indigenous peoples, and, at the same time, to know that it is possible to survive and thrive within the larger society. We may not have had a choice about our bloodline, but we did, and do, have a choice about completing our identities by acquiring heritage. Then and only then can we know and understand the essence of being Indian—an essence that transcends the burden of any labels.

The Myth of the

Hunter/Warrior

or

Men Did the Dangerous Work, Women the Impossible

▲   A prevailing image of Indians among non-Indians is of a
▲   man on a horse, usually with a feather war bonnet and
▲   some kind of weapon in his hands. This archaic, stereo-
▲   typical picture fits primarily the Plains cultures, and it
▲   obscures the lifestyles of other indigenous cultures
across the continent and totally ignores contemporary
Indians. Not all Indians were horse-mounted, nomadic
hunters. Furthermore, this image, although representa-
tive of many Plains tribes, is merely a veneer. It typifies
only one of many societal roles of males and excludes
the roles of females.

The movement of white emigrants across the continent below
the forty-eighth parallel was westward from the eastern seaboard
and northward from the Southwest. Thus the northern Plains
was the last region to feel the pressure of concentrated Euro-
American encroachment, mainly because three of the most significant emigrant trails in the West dissected the region. The
Oregon Trail crossed through the southern portion of Lakota territory in present-day Nebraska and southeastern Wyoming; the
Overland Trail cut across what is now western Nebraska and

southern Wyoming; and the Bozeman Trail traversed from south to north across the Powder River country of central Wyoming, the prime hunting lands of the Oglala Lakota. Any emigrant or military travel on these trails was an outright intrusion to the Lakota. By and large any movement of whites into or across any tribal territories of the Plains was an intrusion so far as the affected tribe was concerned.

Encroachment, intrusion, or outright invasion was eventually countered by resistance. No matter what the tribe—Pawnee, Arapaho, Cheyenne, Lakota, or other—the symbol of that resistance on the Great Plains was the Indian male in the role of warrior. And the image of the Plains Indian fighting man, the warrior or protector, was burned indelibly into the psyche of those emigrants, whether settlers or soldiers, who saw him in action as the angry defender of home and family. It was the only side of the Indian male many whites saw, and circumstances and racial attitudes of the day prohibited whites from experiencing other societal roles filled by Indian men.

If white emigrants moving across the Great Plains saw only one side of the Indian male, they saw even less of the Indian female. Nevertheless, based on limited observations, whites assumed that an Indian woman's lot was one of subservient drudgery. Her purpose, apparently, was to care for the home and family and perform all the menial tasks that were beneath the arrogant man. According to a few white observers, the Plains Indian men did nothing more than father children and laze about in camp while the women did all the work.

Two factors, among others, helped shape white mindset regarding Indians on the Plains. To whites, the land was harsh and unforgiving, with the potential to inflict pain and injury to unsuspecting travelers. In addition, whites assumed there was a constant threat of attack by Indians, whom they saw as living in primitive conditions. Thus Indians were doubly to be feared because they lived in such a harsh environment at a level not much higher than animals, which to the whites was a deplorable way to live.

It must be noted, however, that of the 35,000 emigrant deaths during the Oregon Trail era (10 percent of all travelers over approximately age twenty), significantly less than a thousand resulted from direct conflict with Indians. Yet whites persisted in thinking of Indian men as warlike, bloodthirsty killers, and their wives and mothers as drudges, or squaws. After all, how could they think of primitive, uncivilized men and women still living primarily a Stone Age lifestyle as husbands and wives, fathers and mothers? Yet, Indian men and women had numerous roles in their cultures.

Many of the tribes living on the Great Plains at the time of the first heavy emigrant traffic had been there for hundreds of years, and had thrived in cohesive societies for thousands of years. Any society that survives for generations does so because it has developed definite means and skills to make a living. The best way to make a living during this era was to understand the natural environment, make the best use of what it offered without abusing it, and divide the tasks that contributed to survival and comfort. By the time the first white emigrants started traveling across the Plains, the indigenous peoples had highly developed societies that not only ensured the basic needs of survival but also enabled them to thrive. Having the ability to go beyond mere survival meant that indigenous societies had evolved definite societal roles for men and women, young and old people.

The pre-European cultures of Turtle Island, or North America, had the same basic needs we do today: food, shelter, clothing, and security. Those needs were met by division of labor according to physical capabilities. For practical reasons, men performed tasks women couldn't, while women performed tasks men couldn't. Other tasks could be accomplished by either sex.

Food was procured by hunting, fishing, or gathering. Generally speaking, hunting and fishing were almost exclusively the responsibility of men, while gathering wild fruits and vegetables was frequently done by everyone. Many sedentary tribes planted and raised crops. In some tribes, planting and harvesting were done only by men, in other tribes by women, and in still others they were shared responsibilities.

The Great Plains consisted predominantly of grasslands, with rolling hills and vast prairies as far as the eye could see. To live in such a place, one had to be a wanderer, whether one flew or moved on four legs or two. Over the ages numerous people came to the Great Plains, and although some stayed and some didn't, those who stayed became wanderers, long before the horse arrived. Wandering, migrating was the rhythm, the flow of life on the Plains. To be part of it meant moving with the flow, getting in step with the rhythm. Thus, the two-leggeds who came, stayed, and thrived on the Great Plains were wanderers; their lifestyle was nomadic, and their livelihood was hunting.

The basics of food, shelter, and clothing were supplied by the hunter, which was every male over the age of twelve. Bison, elk, deer, and antelope were the main sources of the basic necessities of life. Hunting and providing for one's family and those in need was a lifelong responsibility. Most of the hunting was done by the younger, more able-bodied men of a household. Once a man was no longer able-bodied enough to withstand the rigors of stalking and chasing, his contribution to the household became wisdom and experience.

Hunting was a necessary activity that demanded much of man's time. The average size of a Plains Indian household was six people, and such a household required from seven hundred to seventeen hundred pounds of fresh meat each year; forty to sixty bison, elk, deer, and antelope hides for clothing and blankets; and another twenty to thirty hides for rawhide to make household items, such as clothing and food containers. While animals were plentiful, they were not passive, and great skill and patience was necessary to hunt them. Bison, elk, deer, and antelope had their own habits, territories, and migration patterns that they followed season after season. Before the hunter could bring down an animal, he had to go where the animal was. And after the animal was down, he had to transport it back to the village or encampment. Hunting, therefore, consumed most of a man's time, perhaps as much as 75 percent of it, leaving the other 25 percent for fulfilling responsibilities as a husband, father, and protector.

The other major societal role of men was that of the protector. The term *warrior* is freely used to describe this role, and although it does apply to an extent, the English definition falls short. A dictionary definition of it is "one who engages in or makes war." By contrast, among many Plains tribes the term *warrior* meant being *a complete man*, one who did the best he could at all times in all endeavors and provided for everyone who depended on him, including those who could not help themselves. So while the man in his role as protector was often called upon to fight an enemy or to engage in war, that was only one aspect of being a warrior.

The man's responsibility as protector was to defend home and family from all enemies. Many of the skills he had—weaponry, marksmanship, and horsemanship, for example—were the same as those required for the hunter. But his *persona* as a fighting man was different from his *persona* as a hunter. Although in each case he was striving to ensure the continuation of life, warfare was much more dangerous and therefore was the one arena in which he could achieve important status in his community with his exploits and accomplishments. Consequently, there was double incentive, if you will, to be more than an adequate fighting man. Many men rose to prominence because of their exploits on the battlefield.

Such men took good advantage of the opportunities available in the dangerous arena of combat to demonstrate the attributes of courage and leadership. Those who died while striving to show courage on the battlefield were assured of being cherished and honored memories. For those who succeeded and survived, achievements in combat became a stepping stone to influence and leadership.

Some men among the Lakota who achieved prominence through bravery in combat were Spotted Tail of the Sicangu Lakota, Red Cloud and Crazy Horse of the Oglala Lakota, and Sitting Bull and Gall of the Hunkpapa Lakota. Each of these leaders established their reputation early as a young fighting man. Spotted Tail went on to become a significant political leader later in life, and it was largely through his diplomacy and leadership that the Sicangu Lakota—now known as the Rosebud Sioux—were able to survive into the twentieth century.

Based on his reputation as a stalwart fighting man, Red Cloud was able to assume a significant leadership role in the 1860s, during what is now called the Bozeman Trail era. It was primarily Red Cloud with whom the peace commissioners of the United States negotiated the Treaty of Horse Creek, otherwise known as the Fort Laramie Treaty of 1868. Largely under Red Cloud's influence and leadership, the Oglala Lakota and their Cheyenne allies forced the abandonment of three military outposts along the Bozeman Trail, which had cut through the Powder River country of what is now north-central Wyoming.

It was during the turbulent Bozeman Trail era that Crazy Horse's growing reputation as a daring fighting man was solidified. In late December of 1866, he led a group of ten decoys who lured Captain William Fetterman and his command of eighty-one soldiers from Fort Phil Kearny (north of present-day Buffalo, Wyoming) into a large, hidden ambush of several hundred Lakota and Cheyenne fighting men. Every soldier was killed in the fight, which lasted less than an hour—known to the Lakota and Cheyenne as the Battle of the Hundred in the Hand and to the whites as the Fetterman Battle. In the ensuing years, Crazy Horse became even more legendary as a war leader, and many looked to him for peacetime leadership as well, a responsibility he accepted reluctantly. In 1876, he was one of the factors in the defeat of the U.S. Seventh Cavalry at the Little Bighorn.

Sitting Bull and Gall were also present at the Battle of the Little Bighorn. In fact, it was due to Sitting Bull's influence that many of the Lakota bands—perhaps as many as eight thousand people—gathered in the valley of the Little Bighorn. He was extremely concerned over the growing presence of whites in Lakota territory and resentful of its consequences, for example the slaughter of bison, diseases, and the establishment of agencies (reservations). He wanted the people to gather and discuss what to do. By 1876, when he was an elder statesman, Sitting Bull's reputation was considerable, he having made his mark as a young fighting man and then solidified his influence as a healer and spiritual leader.

One of Sitting Bull's staunchest supporters, Gall was a very influential man in his own right. In 1876, he was, like Crazy Horse, in his prime, enhancing the reputation and following he had established as a young, seemingly fearless fighting man. Gall's contribution to the defeat of the Seventh Cavalry is often overlooked, mainly because Sitting Bull and Crazy Horse were more famous. Yet it was Gall's tactical leadership which forced Custer's regiment to fight a running battle, during which they had virtually no opportunity to establish defense positions or mount a counterattack. This was the kind of battle that favored the superior horsemanship of the Lakota, which were often referred to as "the finest light cavalry in the world." Sadly, Gall was fighting with a broken heart. Among the first casualties of the fighting, when Major Reno's initial attack was directed at the southern, Hunkpapa end of the encampment along the Greasy Grass, were members of Gall's immediate family, including two of his wives and at least one of his children.

While the exploits of the man as a hunter were not always lauded in song or ceremony, the role of provider was just as necessary as the role of protector. A good hunter's family, it was said, was well clothed and well fed, while a poor hunter's family was dressed shabbily and always hungry. By the same token, the family of a fierce fighting man of high repute slept well at night.

Before the coming of the whites, warfare among the Plains tribes was not as extensive as some writers and historians would have us believe with statements such as "constant warfare." It was easy for nineteenth-century Euro-Americans to assume that every able-bodied Indian male awoke each morning with nothing but warfare on his mind and rode off to find and fight his enemies every day. Such was not the case.

Considering the number of tribes on the Plains, perhaps sixty, and the fact that some tribes were enemies for one reason or another, *someone somewhere* was going off on a horse or revenge raid every day, or seeing to it that territorial boundaries were not being encroached upon. Only in that sense was there constant warfare. Therefore, the Plains Indian fighting man did not live for warfare. While he often took the opportunity to demonstrate courage and fortitude on the battlefield, he didn't constantly look for opportunities to engage in combat.

Every Indian man had a greater variety of roles than hunter and warrior, provider and protector. Throughout his lifetime he was a student, husband, father, grandfather, mentor, healer, spiritualist, military and/or political leader, horse trainer, storyteller, sage, and more. Although not every man performed all these roles, most men fulfilled many of them.

To some extent, of course, personality and aptitude determined the range of roles a man engaged in. Not every man was a good hunter, a skillful warrior, or became a leader. Because of the wide range of human virtues and foibles, some were not wise, and others were not the best husbands or fathers. Perhaps the worst and the best one can say about the Plains Indian male, then as now, is that he was, and is, human.

Whatever a man became in life was due significantly to the influence of others and preordained societal roles. We assume, and rightly so, that older men taught younger ones all of the requisite skills and philosophies to be hunters and fighting men. Yet in the first four to six years of a child's life the women in the immediate household and extended family also had significant influence. In those formative years, both boys and girls were given the foundation that would eventually shape their characters. Much of a boy's interaction during this time was with women—his mother, sisters, aunts, and maternal and paternal grandmothers, as well as women outside the immediate family.

Roles were not always determined strictly by biological factors. Among the Lakota, for example, a child's mother's sister was also addressed as and thought of as *mother*. Likewise, the sister of his maternal and paternal grandmothers was also addressed as and thought of as *grandmother*. Thus, a child could have several mothers and grandmothers, roles that were more than honorary designations. Those who were thought of and addressed as *mother* and *grandmother* actually fulfilled those roles. For example, my maternal grandmother once told me that when she became seriously ill in 1930 soon after my uncle was born and was unable to breastfeed him, her first cousin, who had a baby of her own at the time, breastfed him instead. Therefore, in addition to the usual considerable female influence on any child during the formative years, Lakota women actually fulfilled the role of *mother* to children other than their own biological offspring.

Female influence on a male child during the formative years helped develop the softer sides of his character, such as compassion and thoughtfulness. Moreover, mothers and grandmothers imbued their sons and grandsons with a sense of loyalty and commitment to home and family. And later in life, loyalty and commitment motivated adult men to work hard providing for their families and protecting them with their lives, if necessary.

One virtue taught to all children was strength. It was necessary for all men and women to grow up strong—physically, mentally, and emotionally—to fulfill their societal roles, otherwise the society would fall apart. In teaching this virtue, women were especially significant. Mothers and grandmothers did not preach strength as much as they demonstrated it.

It was often assumed that Indian tribes and cultures were dominated by men. Such an assumption was usually made by white men who liked to think that they were of primary importance in their own society, and that all women were supportive of and subservient to them. However, while some indigenous cultures were male-dominated, many were not, customs that can be substantiated by the fact that in many tribes ancestry was traced through female lineage.

It is important to emphasize that among indigenous tribes there was rarely any sense of competition between genders. After all, life and survival did not depend on such a competition but rather on competition with other forces and powers that affected and threatened existence. On the contrary, the best way to survive and thrive was for everyone to work together, fulfilling necessary roles. Failure to do so weakened the family and community. For example, a hunter's failure to provide the tangible necessity of food meant his family would go hungry. Failure to provide defense and protection put his family and community at great risk. Likewise, if women failed to provide the tangibles of clothing and household accoutrements, the family was uncomfortable or poorly attired. And if women in tribal societies did not fulfill their critical role of childrearing the continuation of the entire society was at risk. Therefore, there was rarely a question of who was most important to the survival and cohesiveness of a society because men knew that their society could not survive and function without women, and vice versa.

Just as men's roles were more varied than whites usually perceived, so were the roles of women. Women did much more than bear children, make clothing, cook, and quill or do beadwork. They were the glue that kept a family together. They were the first storytellers that children heard. They were the first adults with whom children had the most intimate emotional and physical contact—and thus the first role models. The home and family was their domain, and the lodge belonged to them. Beyond that they could be healers, spiritual advisers, herbalists, and so on. Girls were taught the rudiments of weaponry, especially the bow and arrow. If necessary women could hunt, and in some instances they participated as combatants in warfare.

One of the most notable women warriors among the northern Plains tribes was Buffalo Calf Road, the younger sister of a Cheyenne war leader. At the Rosebud Battle on June 17, 1876, she accompanied her brother as part of a large fighting force led by the renowned Lakota war leader Crazy Horse. She participated in the day-long battle during which Crazy Horse's forces brought a larger force commanded by General George Crook to a virtual standstill.

During the battle, her brother's horse was shot out from under him, and he was on foot well within rifle range of a significant soldier position. Buffalo Calf Road rode in amidst a hail of bullets, rescued her brother, and they escaped riding double on her horse. Later, her brother did not hesitate to tell how he had been rescued by his younger sister.

Nevertheless, women combatants were an exception, as were men who assumed roles usually reserved for women. However, while both were societal anomalies, they were nonetheless accepted and tolerated, and in some cases celebrated.

Among many Plains tribes, women's societal role as focal point and nurturer of the family was just as critical to survival as men's role of hunter and fighter. Women were a multigenerational influence on children in the immediate household and the extended family. The physical and practical skills of tracking and shooting the bow taught by male teachers were of no use unless the hunter was also taught loyalty and commitment to the welfare of the family, values usually taught by women. Thus each child was clearly the product of both male and female influence. Among some tribes there was the saying that, "a man learned to hunt and fight from his fathers and grandfathers, but he learned courage from his mothers and grandmothers," a sentiment that sums up the vital importance of women. Furthermore, it was usually the women of a family who supported the bravery of men, frequently reminding the fighting man on the eve of battle that "it is far better to lie a warrior naked on death than to be wrapped up well with a heart of water inside." And in many instances women showed extreme commitment and courage under the most difficult of circumstances.

One example of such courage was demonstrated at the Greasy Grass Fight, or the Battle of the Little Bighorn, when an old woman from the Sicangu band took a young granddaughter by the hand, crossed the Greasy Grass-Little Bighorn-River, and climbed a knoll. This occurred during the engagement where the five companies commanded by Lieutenant Colonel George Custer were being chased toward and along the long rise now known as the Last Stand Ridge. Standing on that knoll, with her granddaughter at her feet, the woman held out her harms and sang strongheart songs and prayed for the Lakota and Cheyenne fighting men. She sang and prayed as long as the fighting lasted, and her presence was noticed by many Indians.

After the battle ended, several warriors came to her and gave her their red sashes. These were fighting men who had pledged their lives to the defense of the people; in combat they had pounded one end of their long sash into the earth, with the other end tied around their waist or ankle, and so tethered would fight until killed or victory was attained. To these experienced warriors fresh from victory over the soldiers, the old woman's show of courage was no less than their own.

Following this battle, the old woman walked back to the encampment with several sashes draped around her shoulders. Later, she took a few strands from each of those sashes and wove them together into a long, red cord, which she braided into her hair. Before she died she gave half of the cord to her granddaughter, who in turn wore it in her hair for the rest of her life, especially whenever she told the story of her grandmother's courage.

In my own upbringing, male and female influence was of equal importance. Raised by my maternal grandparents, I can recall many memorable moments with my grandfather, hunting jackrabbits on the prairies, catching bullheads in the Little White

River, or simply watching him make a bow. Although the lessons I learned from him were invaluable, some of my most profound memories are of interactions with my grandmother. While my grandfather taught me self-sufficiency, my grandmother nurtured my sense of identity and self-esteem, making me feel like I was the most important person in the world.

I know now that both of them were fulfilling roles ancient in origin and appropriate in any time. My grandparents' influence on my life was little different from the influence of grandparents on many Lakota children as far back as memory survives, and beyond. Though my accomplishments will never measure up to those of Spotted Tail, Red Cloud, Crazy Horse, Sitting Bull, or Gall, I do have something in common with them. I am the product of an ancient society whose people not only learned how to survive but refined the ability to thrive; and they did so, not so much by focusing on the inherent differences between men and women, but by finding ways in which men and women could contribute equally to life.

Yet despite these long traditions, sadly, stereotypes of Indians persist in movies, novels, textbooks, and, therefore, in the minds of most non-Indians. Epithets such as *squaw, savage, warlike,* and *drudge* are used in reference to Indian men and women of the past, and sometimes to Indians today. However, such words obscure our humanity and prevent those who believe them from knowing us as we really were, and are. For too many people, the image of an Indian is still of an angry man on a horse with feathers in his hair. Not only is that view narrow, it is also one that is locked in the past.

Today, we Indians, descendants of the indigenous peoples who lived and thrived on this land, are part of the mainstream. Some of us have immersed ourselves completely in the non-Indian culture to the exclusion or obliteration of our heritage. Yet many of us cling tenaciously to our heritage and participate in this society candidly as what we are. All in all, we have survived through trying times and we will continue to survive, as our ancestors did, because of the strength and timelessness of our societies; the values which enabled our ancestors to survive and thrive across the ages still stand us in good stead today.

Of the societal roles among the Plains peoples, the one that has survived mostly intact is that of the women. Their place as the nurturers of family and community, as the wellspring of courage fostered survival during times of change and still persists today. Throughout the turbulent times of change as reservations were established and assimilation threatened our identity as Indians, mothers and grandmothers maintained their ancient role out of necessity. The role of the hunter and protector became nonexistent since the government gave us rations and took away guns, bows, and arrows. While Indian men are still struggling to find a life purpose that will replace the ancient hunter/warrior role, women are maintaining cultural stability as they have for thousands of years. If it were not for them, we would have lost much more of our identities as Lakota, Cheyenne, Pawnee, Comanche, Crow, and so on.

It is impossible to perceive these realities in the image of the man on a horse. Therefore, people must be willing to look beyond that, to see us as men and women, mothers and fathers, grandmothers and grandfathers, teachers, healers, storytellers, successes and failures, winners and losers—as part of the fabric of humankind.

Buffalo Grass

▲   Growing up on the northern Plains I thought that all the
▲   world was a wide expanse of endless prairies and rolling
▲   hills. I couldn't imagine the world being anything but
▲   beckoning open spaces, bright sunrises and spectacular
▲   sunsets, booming, crackling thunderstorms that petrified
the mind and invigorated the spirit. I couldn't picture a
world that didn't know the meadowlark's song, a place
where the wind didn't dance with the grasses. And if
there were such a place, it would never know my footsteps. If there were such a place, surely no one lived
there.

My love for the Plains, my loyalty to them was engen-
dered by the stories my grandparents told because they
and their stories were connected to what the Plains were
and are. Vast, grassy, hot, dry, windy, peaceful, turbulent,
cold, wet, muddy, dusty, ghostly, and motherly. The
Plains were the only home they ever knew in their lives,
and the one I return to as often as I can. And it is where
I will rest when my sojourn in this world is ended.

I have seen the world from mountaintops such as the Gornoi-
Altai region in western Siberia and the Big Horns of the Powder
River Country in north central Wyoming. On the Mojave Desert
I stood and watched heat rise in shimmering, prism waves. Once
I helped a friend build an igloo out of snow in the frozen north

country, and spent a few nights in it. Weaving my way through a dense forest of pine I nearly panicked because there were no horizons to center me. Trekking through a dense tropical jungle I did panic when I couldn't see the sky, only a canopy of green. There was no panic when I played along the seashore with my youngest daughter, perhaps because of the open expanse of Puget Sound. But in all those places I always made a comparison to my home ground.

There is natural beauty everywhere, to be sure. Each kind of terrain, each kind of topography and ecology is unique. But the Plains, especially the northern Plains, are in my heart and in my blood. As unique and beautiful as other wild places are, they will never compare to the Plains.

The Plains made me a wanderer long before I was born. One only needs to know the Plains to know why and how. From the top of one hill I would wonder what was beyond the next highest hill I could see in the distance. And from that hill, there was always another, and another. They all beckoned to come and look. In between the hills were creeks and dry watercourses, gullies, oak and cottonwood groves, chokecherry and buffaloberry shrubs, open meadows, deer, coyotes, rabbits, quail, and butterflies. In between the hills was adventure. Each adventure wove its way into my memory, just as the land and everything, every being that was part of it embedded itself into my heart and connected with the heritage that flowed in my veins. After all, I do come from a long line of wanderers.

The natural environment created the indigenous human cultures of the Turtle Island, on the basis of one simple yet profound lesson. Adapt or perish. Anyone who lived on the Plains had to be a wanderer, or risk death and loneliness. Of course, that was in the time when some humans understood that they had to move with the flow of everything around them.

"Why," I can recall asking my grandparents, "did the people move around so much?"

"Because everything else did," was always the reply.

The influence of nature affected everything. Dwellings, clothing, language, lifestyle, diet, spiritual beliefs and practices, and more, no matter where people lived. Different human cultures evolved because the land was different. Life in the mountains was different from life on the seacoasts or around the great lakes, or the great forests, or the deserts, or the plains. But no matter how many different human cultures there were, they all shared one essential precept: they adapted themselves to fit the natural environment.

It is difficult to know how many peoples came to the Plains in the dim and distant past. Some came of their own accord, others were driven from some other place by change or catastrophe. They all came looking for something, life mostly. Some only passed through and some stayed. Some stayed briefly and some for generations. Some of us are still here. But no one came because they wanted to be wanderers. The land and everything and everyone who was part of the Plains taught them to be wanderers.

The greatest wanderer on the Plains was *tatanka*, the bison, more commonly known as buffalo. *Tatanka* was literally and figuratively the primary source of life for the indigenous people who came and stayed on the Plains. To take advantage of what *tatanka* had to offer the people had to follow the great herds. Thus they became wanderers in order to live.

The buffalo were plentiful. Estimates of their numbers west of the Mississippi River are in the millions, often as high as sixty million; two hundred forty million hooves. And if, on the average, each adult grew to weigh a ton, it's no small wonder that the earth shook when they galloped. One hundred twenty billion pounds on the hoof must have shaken the rafters of the sky itself.

Why, then, did the buffalo wander? Perhaps mainly because they could. There are very few things that can stop a single two-thousand-pound animal, much less a herd of them. I'm convinced that wandering was in the buffalo blood long before humans came to Turtle Island. I hear they originated in northern Europe and I did see their relatives on a farm in Sweden three years ago. Same color, same build, same size, but a little taller at the hip. They are said to have migrated across Asia and then across Berengia to Turtle Island. Once a wanderer, always a wanderer.

On Turtle Island the buffalo found the ideal home on the Plains stretching from what is now central Texas northward to what is now Alberta and Manitoba. Short grass prairie in the west and tall grass prairie in the east, but, most of all, open spaces. Of course other grazing animals lived on the Plains as well. Elk, antelope, and deer. But their numbers combined probably didn't match the buffalo. All of them, of course, were nurtured and sheltered by the land.

When indigenous man finally came to the Plains, he saw that the environment offered all that he could ever need and want for survival. Sooner or later the buffalo became the primary source of food, shelter, and clothing.

One story of the Great Plains prior to the coming of European man is primarily the story of the interrelationship between indigenous man and the buffalo. Indigenous man became and remained dependent on the buffalo, to the point that that dependence became his weakness in the eyes of European man. To weaken and defeat indigenous man, European man eventually annihilated the buffalo. But prior to that both the buffalo and indigenous man flourished. There was more than enough buffalo to feed, shelter, and house all of the population of the Great Plains, because humans probably never numbered more than one-half of one percent of the buffalo population.

Non-Indian anthropologists and others love to talk about the development of the buffalo cultures of the Plains. But some of them link the evolvement of buffalo cultures to the horse. Of course the modern horse was brought to Turtle Island by European man. The not so subtle implication here is that

European man was somehow responsible for creating the buffalo cultures because the horse enabled indigenous man to hunt the buffalo. This shortsightedness ignores the fact that man was hunting buffalo *on foot* long before European man arrived. Furthermore, the Plains people continued to use different methods of hunting buffalo *after* the horse arrived. The point is *buffalo cultures* were in place long before the horse was brought to Turtle Island.

Anyone who knows something about pre-European human cultures on the Plains knows about "buffalo jumps"—drop offs or cliffs over which buffalo were chased and fell to their death. That is the most widely known method of buffalo-hunting prior to horse-mounted chases. Other popular methods involved wolves, snow, and practicality.

One or two wolves were not considered a significant threat to a herd of buffalo. Both the buffalo and the wolves knew that, and so did indigenous man. Therefore, by draping a wolf hide over his body, a single hunter—or sometimes two—could crawl on hands and knees to within easy bow shot of a small herd. When the right opportunity presented itself, the hunter loosed several arrows into one animal and crawled away to wait for the stricken buffalo to die from bleeding.

Hunting was not a seasonal sport, of course, it was done year round. Winter hunting on the Plains was the most difficult for the obvious reasons of cold and snow. But deep snow became an ally of indigenous man after he figured out how to make snowshoes to keep him from sinking in. On the other hand the buffalo's great weight was a liability in deep snow. Small groups of hunters on snowshoes would look for buffalo digging for browse in sheltered areas, then drive them into deep snow. As the buffalo floundered, their size and speed were neutralized and the hunters would move in with bows and arrows. A few daring ones moved in close enough to use a lance.

Another effective year-round method was the ambush. Pits were dug or blinds were built along known buffalo routes. The hunter, or hunters, would hide and wait for a close shot at a passing animal, letting it quarter away from him for the best shot.

The horse, therefore, was not an instrument of change. It was a tool to enhance an already existing lifestyle. Most of the indigenous tribes of the Plains were nomads—wanderers—before the horse came. The horse simply enabled them to travel farther and faster and carry bigger loads.

The buffalo cultures were more than indigenous man's material dependence on the buffalo. But because he was grateful for all that the buffalo provided, he gave the buffalo the only thing he could: respect.

For the sake of practicality indigenous man's respect for the buffalo led him to utilize everything the buffalo had to offer. Little, if anything, was wasted. The trademark of the Plains tribes—the conical lodge—was made of twenty to twenty-five scraped and treated buffalo hides. With the winter hair left on and tanned on the other side, they were the warm winter robes. The hair was twisted into cordage, ropes and tie downs to help secure the lodge, and for reins (jaw ropes) and war bridles for the horses. Hooves were boiled to make glue. Bones were used for toys, utensils, weapons, and sled runners. Horns were fashioned into cups, ladles, and spoons. The tips were used to make necklaces. Sinew—both backstrap and hamstring—was used as bowstrings and fletching wrap on arrows. The list goes on and on.

As a symbolic gesture of respect a buffalo skull was placed to face the east, to greet the rising sun each day. And of course the buffalo was given significant roles in origin stories. According to one Lakota story, the Lakota at one time lived underground beneath the *Paha Sapa*—the Black Hills. They were enticed to go above ground and so they emerged from a cave, but once they had emerged they could not return. A leader stayed underground, however, because he foresaw hardship for the people. When that hardship did occur he sacrificed his own safety and emerged onto the Earth in the form of a buffalo. And, of course, the buffalo became the source for all the necessities of life for the Lakota, enabling them to live through the hardships and become prosperous.

A more well-known story is about the White Buffalo Calf Maiden. Because of hardships faced by the people, a female white buffalo appeared in the form of a beautiful woman and brought sacred ceremonies to the people. She taught them the ceremonies and left. Leaving, she walked into a mist and reappeared on the other side as a white buffalo.

Sitting on the fringes of a conversation among old Lakota men once when I was a boy, I heard a story that is one of my favorites. It was a story of an actual occurrence.

That conversation, as I recall, was about the old life before the reservation, when the Lakota still lived on the land and moved with the seasons. It was about a time when there were still wolves and bears in what is now south central South Dakota, and, of course, many, many buffalo.

Two rivers meet in that part of the country and they are now known as the Big White and Little White Rivers. The old men who told the story called the Big White the White Earth River and the Little White the Smoking Earth River. The Smoking Earth/Little White River flows into the Big White/White Earth River, which in turn flows into the Big Muddy or Missouri River.

At the confluence of the Smoking Earth and White Earth Rivers was a trading site. Early French traders traveled up from the Big Muddy with their trade goods. The Lakota who were inclined to trade traveled from their various encampments and pitched their lodges at the trading site. One such group was on a high ridge overlooking the confluence, waiting for a large buffalo herd to pass. The herd was traveling to the northeast. Suddenly another large herd came from the northwest, heading in a southeasterly direction. The two herds met at a crossing just west of the confluence, and each herd was strung out for two to three miles, according to the storytellers.

The Lakota travelers on the ridge watched as the two herds met, expecting to see some confusion as the herds began to mingle. The animals crossed the river leisurely, dropped their great heads to water, and then moved on. There was no confusion.

Instead the two herds crisscrossed each other and eventually continued on their individual courses, one to the southeast and the other to the northeast.

This took place in the early 1800s and the story was handed down from the Lakota travelers who witnessed the occurrence.

The buffalo, and to a lesser degree elk, deer, and antelope, provided for the physical and spiritual survival of the people of the Plains, like the Lakota. What, then, did the buffalo survive on? Obviously their requirements for survival were provided by the resources of the Plains, otherwise they would not have flourished.

Forage in the form of several kinds of grasses was plentiful on the Plains, such as chufa, sedge, cottongrass, spikegrass, reedgrass, june grass, needle grass, gramma, and, of course, buffalo grass.

Strangely enough, buffalo grass was not as widespread as some of the other types of forage. It is a short grass still found in a narrow corridor from Texas to Canada that seems to coincide with the geographical boundaries of the Great Plains.

Buffalo grass was important forage for buffalo, but not exclusively as the name might suggest. But however the name came about, it does suggest a unique, symbiotic relationship between it and its namesake.

One Lakota word for buffalo grass is *peji iwicakoyake*, or grass-that-catches. The name was applied because of the creeping runners just beneath the soil surface between main stalks or clumps. Someone walking would often catch their toe on the runners; thus the name. And that someone walking could be man or animal. This characteristic meant survival for the grass and was the basis for the relationship between it and the buffalo.

Buffalo roamed in large and small herds and they were especially active from mid-spring to early autumn, the period when buffalo grass flourished. To be sure buffalo ate buffalo grass, but they also helped replant. The front animals in large herds moving swiftly would knock down seeds and the ones coming behind would push them into the ground.

It is interesting to note that buffalo grass was plentiful on the open prairies of the Great Plains, in the area with the largest concentrations of buffalo. Buffalo grass hardly grows anywhere else on the continent.

I would suggest, however unscientifically, that though buffalo grass is still found on the Great Plains it is not nearly as plentiful as when buffalo roamed the land by the millions. In fact it grew so thick that early white settlers took advantage of its soil-binding properties by cutting it into slabs to make sod houses.

The other reason buffalo grass and buffalo are not as plentiful as they once were is that modern man has taken over much of their space. Roads, towns, and cities proliferate, obliterating the migratory routes of the buffalo. Whatever open grazing land remains is set aside for domesticated cattle and sheep. Cultivated crops have shouldered aside the native flora in much the same way indigenous people were overwhelmed by the larger European and Euro-American population.

Right or wrong, destiny or coincidence, change is a part of life and it is no more or no less true for all who were a part of the Great Plains, including the land itself. But change on the Plains has moved at a swifter faster pace in the last three hundred years than it had in the previous few thousand years.

Twenty-five million people now call the Plains home and buffalo number less than one percent of the human population. They are feared by cattle producers because they are brucellosis carriers, a disease which can cause spontaneous abortion in domestic cattle. The fear is so great that buffalo wandering out of the boundaries of Yellowstone National Park are summarily shot. It's doubtful that the buffalo killers remember that domestic cattle infected buffalo with brucellosis. Perhaps some effort should be put forth to determine why buffalo are not as radically affected by the disease. Perhaps killing buffalo is too ingrained in the Euro-American mind, or perhaps some may think that the act of killing is the only answer.

The Plains will never be the same, which of course is the first law of change: nothing remains the same. Wolves no longer inhabit the Plains because they were victims of unfounded fears, and the knee-jerk reaction to eradicate the fears was to eradicate the wolf. Grizzly bears are gone from the Plains, too, partly due to extirpation but mostly because of loss of habitat. Towns, farms, ranches, and roads invaded their territory and people became too numerous. We indigenous peoples are still here. But our populations had to rebound from the brink of extinction. Around 1900 our total population in the United States was just over two hundred thousand, lower than the indigenous Plains population alone at the moment of first contact with European man. Estimates of our total North American population around 1500 A.D. range from three to ten million. Fortunately, those of us on the Plains seem to be as resilient as buffalo grass.

Hunting was the predominant source of survival and livelihood on the Plains prior to European man's arrival. Agriculture has taken its place now and hunting is a seasonal sport. In fact the Great Plains are now referred to as The Breadbasket in Joel Garreau's 1981 book *The Nine Nations of North America*. Ironically, the farming lifestyle so detested and resisted by the nomadic hunting tribes now prevails.

The cycles of nature still come and go, however. The lightning still flashes, the thunder still booms. Blizzards still howl across the landscape. Meadowlarks still sing and the wind still dances with the grass. Against all odds the natural environment of the Plains remains true to itself, in spite of the fact that the new humans who inhabit it are not as adaptive as they are manipulative. We have forgotten the adapt or perish edict and endeavor to change the land to fit our wants, our needs, and our whims—farm-to-market roads, hydroelectric dams, flood walls, and recreation areas, for example. There are still wanderers, of sorts, but they crisscross the land on paved roads riding inside climate-controlled conveyances, hardly ever stopping to feel the soil, touch the grass, or feel the wind on their faces.

The Great Plains will outlive us two-leggeds, as it always has.

I pray that it can overcome the scars we have left due to our arrogance and disrespect. After all, we nearly killed the land once by plowing it so much that we stripped it faster than it could renew itself. The winds came and turned the world into clouds of dust, trying to remind us that technology and industry are not the same as wisdom.

The great rivers of the Plains flooded recently, reminding us of the awesome power of the natural environment. Some of us were outraged and insulted and amidst the subsequent wailing were the catch phrases "the ravages of nature," "nature's cruelty," and "battling the elements." We measured our losses in terms of millions and billions of dollars and vowed to rebuild, to dig in, to build stronger retaining walls so that the next time nature "oversteps its bounds" we can put up a better fight. But, why fight? Why do we insist on characterizing our relationship with nature as a contest? Perhaps because we consider ourselves as being apart from it and on a higher level. As long as we continue to think that way the natural environment will continue to whip our butts.

The Great Plains have changed because, if nothing else, we have multiplied alarmingly. But along with that we have largely forgotten how to adapt to the land. We continue to build homes and towns in flood plains, we overplow, overplant, and overgraze. Our arrogance leads us to think that nature sends tornadoes, floods, and blizzards exclusively to bedevil us. Damages from such natural occurrences are measured in terms of how humans are affected. We seldom consider that wild or domestic animals are also injured or killed, or that the trees uprooted in a storm will die, or that the earth, rivers, lakes, and streams are also affected. The arrogance is equaled only by its narrow scope.

Our hold on the Plains will remain as it is because we think that change is only a forward motion. We become indignant at the thought of going back because we think in terms of improvement and less often of restoration. I can recall the angry outcries some years ago when it was suggested that public lands should be used to restore the buffalo to the Plains.

We are more likely to put up new fences than tear down old ones because we define the land as commodity, not as a living entity. We are reluctant to consider that the wisdom of the past helped the indigenous people to adapt to the land, to move with its rhythms and cycles instead of competing with it. It is a lesson we don't want to consider because it seems to mean going backward. That attitude prevents us from realizing that moving with the natural environment is really a step forward. If we take the responsibility to see to it that the land will endure and survive, we are ensuring our own survival.

Whatever our culture, those of us who are from the Plains, or have lived there, are profoundly affected by them. We are either in love with the open spaces or we consider them empty. Rarely is there ambivalence. As has always been the case, some of us belong on the Plains and some of us don't. But the factors which now bring us here, keep us here, or cause us to leave are often not directly related to the natural environment. More than likely they are money or career. And that turns out to be a losing situation for us and the environment. Whatever it is that prevents us from having a close, profound relationship with the natural Plains or the environment of any other culture area, creates an artificial, often superficial buffer that manipulates us into thinking of ourselves as more important than that environment. We are part of a whole, not an entity apart from it.

The Plains no longer shudder from the thunder of millions of buffalo. Yet the land is still alive, and it will endure all the insults we have managed to heap upon it. Whatever we have done to it there is one final reality: in the end it will claim us all. Some of us will feel a welcome embrace. Some of us will only feel the cold.

White Lore

▲   On the whole I believe that the average Indian person in
▲   the United States knows more about white society than
▲   the average white person knows about Indians.
▲   Assimilation and acculturation have seen to that.
▲   Assimilation is forced change, the process used by
the federal government in the late 1800s and early
1900s—with the active support of many Christian
churches—to try to force us to be white. Acculturation,
on the other hand, was the mechanism we preferred
(and still do) since it is the process of learning and
adapting by choice and not coercion. As a result, some of
us have chosen to divest ourselves of our native heritage.
Many of us, however, do hang onto it for dear life, choos-
ing to adapt without giving up our core ethnic identity.
But the bottom line is that most white people have not
had to survive in Indian society the way Indians have
had to survive in white society. Although there are whites
who live on or near reservations, too many of them,
while lamenting or boasting of the experience, don't
truly understand it.

Of course, there are whites who have a deep, abiding, sincere
interest in us and take the trouble to learn what they can,
although these are few in number. Fewer still are whites who
learn about Indians directly from Indians. But the surprising

consequence of all this is how a few white people can draw such erroneous conclusions, and even write articles, scholarly papers, stories, and books about us, based on limited, often biased, and mostly false information. I think I know the basis for this problem: Whites who do learn about Indians get most of their information from books—books written mostly by whites. Therein lies the rub. Never have so few misled so many based on so little accurate information.

Indians are in thousands of books. Paintings and photographs of our faces, figures, accoutrements, clothing, and dwellings fill coffee table and reference books. Our customs, traditions, spiritual rituals, lifestyles, and languages are depicted or described in novels, encyclopedias, and scholarly works.

While some non-Indian authors writing about Indians do go directly to the source during their research—that is, to Indians with knowledge—too many rely on non-Indian observations. The consequences of such incomplete research are the perpetuation of inaccurate information about Indian culture and history and unrealistic representations of the Indian mindset. Thus, people who are looking for facts and reality about Indians are apt to get misinformation.

Recently, for example, I perused a book about the "Teton Sioux," in which the author mistakenly identified the "Teton Sioux" as one of the seven bands of the Western Sioux, or Lakota. In reality, the Anglicized term *teton* is derived from the Lakota word *titunwan*, which refers to all of the seven bands of the Lakota and means "those who live on the prairies." *Titunwan* is not applied to the Dakota or Nakota, the two eastern groups of the nation that live east of the Missouri River. The third group, the Lakota, live on the prairies west of the Missouri River.

Similarly, in an ethnological study I saw several references to Sitting Bull as a Dakota. While there were other Indians with the same name, the Sitting Bull who was largely responsible for the coalition at the Little Bighorn in 1876 that defeated the U.S. Seventh Cavalry was a *Hunkpapa Lakota*. To confuse the issue further, I came across a lengthy explanation rationalizing the frequent use of the term *Dakota* as a reference to the nation comprised of the Nakota, Dakota, and Lakota. By and large it said that it was easier for whites to think of the three linguistic and geographic divisions of the nation by one word: *Dakota*. And even in the popular biography of Crazy Horse by Mari Sandoz, the word *Dakota* is used in reference to the Lakota.

These are small errors perhaps, but they are the foundation for misinformation and could be easily avoided by going to the proper source. If you want to know about Indians, go to Indians who know. And by all means avoid anyone, Indian or white, who claims to have extensive knowledge of Indian lore.

Any claim or reference to *extensive knowledge* should be met with skepticism in the interest of reality and self-preservation. Extensive knowledge seems to propagate titles such as *The Last of the Mohicans* and *The Last Days of the Sioux Nation*. Contrary to the implications in such titles, Mohicans, or Mahicans, as well as the Sioux (Dakota, Nakota, and Lakota) are still alive and kicking.

Though I would like to think otherwise, writers are no more or less prone to error than any other group. Unfortunately, our mistakes are sometimes published, and once something is in print it tends to become gospel. But it is especially worrisome when someone fashions a story based on his or her extensive knowledge of Indian lore or makes conclusions based on subjective observations of Indians. Moreover, when such a person has a considerable reputation and following or a work becomes a "classic," the information conveyed becomes truth, no matter how subjective, ludicrous, or fictitious. Such is the case, I believe, with two books: *Last of the Breed* by Louie L'Amour, published in 1986, and *The Oregon Trail* by Francis Parkman, Jr., published in 1840. Louie L'Amour wrote his book based on his extensive knowledge of Indian lore, while Parkman's work is regarded by non-Indians as a classic on Indian lore. One gives incorrect historical and cultural information, and the other makes erroneous conclusions on Indian life.

Last of the Breed is a well-written contemporary novel, and my criticism is not of L'Amour's ability to weave a story. The interesting plot develops around an American pilot captured by the Russians in an attempt to extract information about new American aircraft. The pilot, who is part Sioux and part Cheyenne with a little Scottish thrown in for effect, escapes from a Siberian prison camp as winter approaches and must use his knowledge of primitive Sioux culture to survive and escape his pursuers.

My first bone of contention is with the title. *Last of the Breed* implies that the protagonist, Major Joseph Makatozi, is the last of his kind to possess the knowledge and abilities to do what the character does in the story. Makatozi resorts to his primitive heritage to live off the land and deal with his enemies, making a bow and arrows, hunting, tanning hides, and crafting moccasins. While most Indian men today will probably never find themselves in such a predicament as L'Amour's hero, that does not preclude the reality that some of us have specific tribal knowledge of weaponry and primitive skills, not to mention the philosophies associated with being a real warrior—the definition of which is being *a complete man* as opposed to the popular definition of *one who makes or wages war*. Furthermore, we will not be the last of the breed simply because, true to Indian oral tradition, some of us pass on our knowledge to sons, daughters, and grandchildren.

Of course, L'Amour implies that his hero is the last of his breed because he never lived on a reservation, thereby apparently untainted by the influences of reservation Indians. Still, the title has subtle, erroneous implications.

However, the title's false implications are not as damaging as the characterization of the hero as an "unreconstructed savage," a description intended by L'Amour to reflect Makatozi's ability to survive in a hostile land, and elude or kill his enemies. To me, savagery, as well as nobility, is defined by actions and attitudes rather than race or ethnicity. Interestingly, when L'Amour describes the hero's Scottish ancestors as "bloodying their claymores" in combat against their enemies, he does not characterize that behavior as savage. Yet there seems to be little doubt that Makatozi is "an unreconstructed savage" due to his Sioux and Cheyenne ancestry.

Basically, L'Amour's protagonist is knowledgeable about his ancestral background, but the numerous references to historical events, figures, and ancient Sioux societal values are presented according to L'Amour's perspective, which did not always correspond to reality.

For example, L'Amour describes Crazy Horse, the legendary Oglala Lakota warrior, as having gray eyes, obviously placing some stock in the theory that the man was part white. In another instance, he chooses not to tell the entire story regarding an actual incident involving the Hunkpapa Lakota Rain-in-the-Face. In reality, Crazy Horse's mother was a Mniconju Lakota, and his father was Oglala Lakota. He was raised largely in the Oglala community, and after his biological mother died, his father married two Sicangu Lakota sisters. Therefore, he was biologically and ethnically Lakota. It was, and is, not unusual for recessive physiological anomalies to appear among dark-skinned peoples, such as Crazy Horse's dark brown, wavy hair and possibly slightly lighter than usual skin. Such characteristics are largely overlooked by white observers unless the individual possessing them is a prominent figure. The apparent assumption on the part of white historians and writers focusing on Crazy Horse's appearance is to imply that he would not have been capable of his considerable achievements without some white blood in his veins.

Rain-in-the-Face, along with a companion, was taken prisoner by soldiers from Fort Abraham Lincoln (near present-day Bismark, North Dakota) as suspects in an alleged offense against a white family. During their imprisonment, Rain-in-the-Face and his companion were beaten by soldiers while their hands were bound.

L'Amour uses the incident to establish that Rain-in-the-Face developed a healthy respect for Captain Tom Custer, purporting that Custer physically overpowered Rain-in-the-Face. Rain-in-the-Face and his companion reported that the officer in charge, Tom Custer, ordered soldiers to beat them. There was no man-to-man confrontation between the two men. Yet L'Amour describes how, during the Battle of the Little Bighorn in June 1876, Rain-in-the-Face stalked Tom Custer during the battle and ate his heart after the soldier was killed. This happened because, according to L'Amour, Rain-in-the-Face respected Tom Custer's bravery and wanted to acquire that bravery by eating his heart.

There are several errors in L'Amour's version of the Rain-in-the-Face/Tom Custer incident. Apparently L'Amour chose to use only official army reports in his depiction of the incident in *Last of the Breed*, totally ignoring Rain-in-the-Face's version, corroborated by his companion. First, Rain-in-the-Face detested Tom Custer because the officer did not confront or face him man-to-man at Fort Abraham Lincoln. Second, the Lakota and Cheyenne camped on the Little Bighorn were not certain, and didn't care, which army unit was attacking them. Therefore, Rain-in-the-Face could not have known it was Tom Custer's regiment and would not have looked for him during the battle. It was only after the battle that George Custer was recognized by some Cheyenne women, and Rain-in-the-Face thereby deduced that the soldiers were from the fort where he had been imprisoned. By design or by accident, he did find the body of Tom Custer and mutilated it, inflicting the most grievous insult he could think of on an enemy he detested.

Undeniably, L'Amour does know something about Indians and draws on that information to weave his story in *Last of the Breed*. However, although he creates a fascinating character and a fast-moving plot, he also portrays a white man's Indian. L'Amour apparently didn't think that contemporary Indians were in touch with their past cultures and values. His protagonist ponders, at one point, if he is the last Indian to live the old way and "think the old thoughts." In reality, many of us think the old thoughts and unabashedly wish that things were different, even as they once were before the coming of white men. And although we no longer reside in buffalo hide tipis, tule reed lodges, or longhouses, many of us still try to live by the values which have survived through the ages—values such as respect for the elderly and the extended family, in connection with which we have never forgotten that it takes a whole village to raise a child. And unlike L'Amour's protagonist, many Indians today endeavor to maintain those values on a daily basis. It is clear that the hero Makatozi is a white man's Indian. He is proud of his place in the white man's world because he does not live in it as an Indian, he lives in it as a white man. He—and therefore L'Amour—did not understand that it is much harder to live in the white man's world as an Indian.

Despite its inaccuracies, ironically *Last of the Breed* does seem to be an unintentional metaphor. Just as Makatozi found himself in a hostile environment in a foreign land, too many times we Indians find ourselves in the same situation—although not in a foreign land. Often we face considerable hostility in our own communities and reservations. And we are forced to rely on the ancient values which make us what we are—such as patience, courage, and fortitude—in order to survive difficult moments and episodes. Thus, while Makatozi experiences a once-in-a-lifetime adventure, for many of us real Indians, facing hostility is a lifelong problem.

The Oregon Trail, parts of which were first published in 1849 with revisions as late as 1892, is an account of Francis Parkman, Jr.'s journey across the American West for several months in 1846.

The 1840s was a period of turmoil for the tribes west of the Mississippi River, especially those on the Great Plains. Control of western lands was the central issue between the Euro-American nation experiencing growing pains and the various tribes, such as the Pawnee, Arapaho, Cheyenne, and Sioux.

Other tribes, including the Kansa, Sauk and Fox, Iowa, and Osage, were already reeling from the effects of civilization, for the most part already having yielded to the unrelenting push of "manifest destiny."

Parkman's journey began along the route of the Oregon Trail and eventually doubled back along the Santa Fe Trail, ending in Westport, Missouri, where it began. He traveled over two thousand miles over five months, one week, and two days.

The first time I read *The Oregon Trail* I was both envious and angry. I envied Parkman his adventure, feeling (as a much younger man then) that I would probably never have an adventure of such magnitude. And, although I've been on several memorable journeys of my own since then, I'm still angry with Parkman. I'm angry for two reasons. First, Parkman could not see beyond the attitudes toward and opinions of Indians held by most Americans of the day. Second, he expressed them. I have no quarrel with Parkman's right to express himself, only with his narrowmindedness.

Parkman traveled across a land populated by peoples whose societies predated his own on this land by thousands and thousands of years. He thus had a unique opportunity to add numerous facts to the body of information Euro-Americans had on indigenous peoples—an opportunity to test myth against reality, to breach the barriers of bigotry and religious intolerance, and to understand how indigenous people thrived in the natural environment while Euro-Americans struggled. However, Parkman didn't take advantage of this opportunity because he was neither a scholar nor an unbiased observer. He was simply an adventurer who didn't have the understanding or the ability to see the potential of contributing to human knowledge. But even if he had recognized his opportunity, he probably would not have taken advantage of it because he was a product of a society that saw itself as the pinnacle of human civilization. By contrast, the various groups and tribes Parkman saw on his journey were regarded as inferior, if they were regarded as human at all. Unfortunately for Parkman and for history, he was merely a traveler who did not understand the road he had traveled.

I don't blame Parkman for who he was, any more than I blame myself for who I am. Yet who we are is important because as individuals, groups, or races, and as proponents of any philosophy, it is the first step in the process of building relationships. It is what we have to offer to the world. But who we are is more often a stumbling block than a stepping stone because we frequently use our often overrated assessment of ourselves as a skewed standard to measure others. And, of course, whoever we are judging invariably is found lacking because we further complicate the situation by confusing difference with quality. In other words, we see something or someone who is different from us and decide that they are less than or not quite as good as us. One wonders what the state of the world would be if we— as individuals, groups, and nations—could more often be unbiased observers and truly accept others for who they are rather than how they fail to measure up in comparison with us.

Parkman had a unique opportunity to briefly step away from his Christian, Euro-American identity and live his adventure free of prejudice and bias. Thus unhampered by the necessity to judge and make comparisons, he might have looked at both the land and the peoples he met through unbiased eyes and truly learned. Perhaps then he might have accepted reality rather than assessing it or altering it to fit his values and beliefs.

Instead, unfortunately Parkman's perspective prevented him from testing myth against reality, and he thereby strengthened the barriers of bigotry and religious intolerance rather than breaching them. For example, he did not consider the possibility that the indigenous peoples he saw had anything to teach civilized society regarding how to live with the natural environment. And, of course, he did nothing to ease the turmoil of that period for either side in the so-called clash of cultures.

By contrast, Parkman did further the cause of "manifest destiny" since his book served to reaffirm ethnocentric Euro-

American opinions of the natives of North America. *The Oregon Trail* did not, and could not, improve the relationship between whites and Indians because Parkman himself saw no advantage, or profit, in that possibility. Instead, he chose to be a populist, and his book became another acrimonious wedge in the clash of cultures rather than a bridge between two races of people. It is unfortunate that his adventure could not have been at least a small stepping stone toward understanding.

Today *The Oregon Trail* is regarded still by Euro-Americans as an important work. However, this record of one man's journey, of a human experience, remains flawed by ethnocentrism. All Indians I personally know who have read *The Oregon Trail* have either mixed feelings or negative opinions of the book. To me, it is primarily another book that contributes to misnomers, misinformation, and stereotypes.

In discussing such books as *Last of the Breed* and *The Oregon Trail* it is interesting to raise the question of whether they are beneficial or harmful in a larger context. Both, I think. There is a natural tendency for anyone interested in Indians to seek insight and information from someone who is considered knowledgeable, someone whom they trust. Louie L'Amour and Francis Parkman, Jr. certainly fit the bill for non-Indians. However, non-Indians tend to overlook the fact that while L'Amour and Parkman may have extensive knowledge of Indian lore and may have lived an adventure which put them face-to-face with Indians, they did not—and probably could not—live the reality of being Indian, now or in the 1840s. The positive aspect of their work about Indians is that it provides a way to pique the curiosity about Indian culture and can serve as a starting point for anyone searching for Indian reality from Indians.

At the same time, however, such works can be harmful if people believe that Louie L'Amour and Francis Parkman, Jr. know more about Indians than even the most knowledgeable Indians. It forces us Indians to deal with the white man's Indian versus what we really are.

For example, L'Amour created a hero that he was comfortable with, which is every novelist's prerogative. However, more than likely the hero reflects the type of Indian that was most acceptable to him in real life. Someone like Makatozi is okay because he is college-educated and a jet pilot serving in the military. Indians like the character Makatozi do exist and are accepted into white society because they have attained a comfort level, if you will. They have pulled themselves up to be reasonable facsimiles of whites, and, hence, more acceptable. And whites often feel, both consciously and subconsciously, more comfortable with that type of Indian—a white man's Indian. However, they either don't realize that the price of being a white man's Indian is the suppression of one's ethnicity or they believe this is a necessary sacrifice.

In connection with this notion of loss of identity, although Parkman felt pity for Indians he perceived as destitute because they did not have what he had, he believed that the destiny of Indians was to be overwhelmed by the push of progress and civilization. Consequently, in Parkman's work we see another kind of white man's Indian—the sacrificial lamb clearly inferior to whites.

Another kind of white man's Indian portrayed by Parkman is based on his belief that anyone who is considered inferior can be improved by associating with someone who is judged superior. This attitude influences certain scenes among the Lakota. For example, on one occasion Parkman comments on his being a guest in a Lakota lodge, assuring the reader that his cavalier way of inviting himself into a lodge was quite acceptable to the hosts because Indians, by and large, were quite honored to have any white man in their home. Parkman had no inkling that his hosts were too polite to ask him to leave, and that putting up with an intrusive and arrogant guest was preferable to breaking a long-standing tradition of courtesy to guests, whether invited or uninvited. (I would give anything to be able to travel back in time to that Lakota lodge and listen to the conversation just after

Parkman had left.)

Somewhere in between L'Amour's depictions based on extensive knowledge and Parkman's portrayals based on subjective observations lies the truth about Indians, historically and contemporarily. Like it or not, we have been and are a part of American society—a society that still tries to assimilate us but into which we have been slowly acculturating ourselves. At this point, in spite of the occasional non-Indian uprising of interest in us, we still know more about white society than white society may ever hope to know about us. But we have more than extensive knowledge, we have insights into the larger society. We know more about white lore than whites know about Indian lore.

We have walked the white man's road because it was necessary for the survival of our languages, values, spiritual beliefs, customs, and traditions, and ourselves. We have endured assimilation and chose acculturation not because the larger society was better, but because adapting was necessary for our survival. Who we are, tempered by the difficulties of the past five hundred years, is our gift to the world. If the world wants to accept this gift, it is best given directly rather than through the diffusive filters of extensive knowledge and subjective observations. In short, we know ourselves better than anyone can. What's more, we are a reputable source on white lore.

Lure of the Holy Iron

▲   People are drawn to weapons, especially males. It's rare
▲   that a male, young or old, can resist connecting with a
▲   weapon, to at least caress the lines, angles, and curves of
▲   a rifle or a handgun with a lingering, covetous, some-
▲   times loving gaze. The next step is to touch it, heft it,
gauge its weight and balance, to feel the awfulness of its
potential.

    Weapons have been a part of human existence since
time immemorial. They have been critical to the attain-
ment and provision of the human need for food, shelter,
and security. They mesh with our predatory nature,
sometimes feeding it. Furthermore, when our basic
needs are satisfied or our environment can no longer
supply them, with weapons in hand and driven by need,
want, or impulse, we become imperialistic. Too often we
do so solely for the sake of being such, our attitudes bol-
stered by the size and number of our weaponry. Such
patterns of human behavior, with little variation, have
occurred across the world.

Improvements in the effectiveness of weaponry have given definite advantage to those whose technology was quicker to bring
them about. But too often we focus on making something bigger, faster, or better without considering the consequences. If our
ability to understand the impact of change correlated with our

ability to use technology, history might have been different. The rapid growth of technology outstripped our societal values in the beginning, and then it began to create new ones. Unfortunately, technology continues to move much faster than our ability to assess its impact on our psyche. This is most destructive in the arena of weaponry because weapons too often appeal to the darker sides of human nature. A popular saying in the late nineteenth century American West was "God created man but Colonel Colt mad them equal." This, of course, in reference to the Colt six-shot revolver. In other words, what a man lacked in resolve, ability, physical stature, reputation, or courage could be circumvented when he took up a weapon. The weapon was, in many cases, more important than the man. That attitude was introduced to the indigenous peoples of this continent along with the European firearm.

That attitude also took hold among the indigenous peoples who acquired the firearm. And while many non-Indian historians and writers glibly proclaim—for ethnocentric reasons—that "the gun conquered the West," the firearm had an influence beyond the battlefield. It occurred within the man who used the firearm. It still occurs.

As a child listening to stories told by my maternal grandparents and others of that generation, I asked a few times why things had to turn out the way they did. The most frequent answer, often given with a sad shake of a gray head, was "there were too many of them."

Never did my grandparents or others say that things turned out the way they did because the whites were a better people. Being realists, however, they did acknowledge that there were good people among the whites. And, good or bad, the whites had goods that were desirable: cloth, coffee, matches, iron axes, iron needles, kerosene lamps, and scissors, for example. They used the practical things that made tasks and everyday life easier, wondering how a people that could produce such good and useful things were not always good and useful themselves.

My grandparents were of the first generation among most of the Lakota to be born into the reservation era. The Rosebud Sioux Indian Reservation—first known as the Spotted Tail Agency—was established around 1889. Though cultural memories of the nomadic hunting lifestyle were still vivid and strong, the reality of their situation could not be avoided. Their parents had adapted to changing times because it was necessary, not because it was desirable. It was a painful lesson to pass on.

My grandparents, therefore, were born into a world firmly controlled by whites and into a lifestyle reluctantly in transition. Lakota families lived in square houses, rode in buckboards, used candles and kerosene lamps for light, kept track of time with clocks, and hung calendars on their walls, among other things. But often next to the square house was a tipi, albeit made of canvas. Yet that tipi was nothing more than a wistful and wishful connection to the past. The old lifestyle was gone. Many of the old ways, values, and societal roles were gone forever or altered significantly.

Reservations imposed a restricted lifestyle especially in terms of territory and activity. Regular issue of government annuities, much of it food, meant that the hunting lifestyle was gone. The male as the hunter/provider was no longer necessary. Furthermore, establishment of reservations meant that the war against the encroachment and invasion of whites had been lost. Consequently there was no further need of the male as the warrior/protector.

To be sure many Lakota men augmented the government food issues by hunting deer or small game. But the grand blood-boiling, heart-stopping tradition of riding after the bison was forever gone. So, too, were legendary fighting men such as Crazy Horse and Spotted Tail.

For all practical purposes the *hunter/warrior* was gone. His final demise came with the establishment of the reservation, but it began nearly two hundred years before with the appearance of firearms.

No one knows precisely when any kind of a firearm first became known to the Lakota. We do know, however, that while the Lakota, Nakota, and Dakota were still in the lakes region of what is now Minnesota, the French traded or provided firearms to the Ojibway who used their weapons to drive us westward. So as early as 1700, or perhaps before, we Lakota were aware of firearms and their awful capability.

In the late 1720s and early 1730s, a Frenchman, the Sieur de la Verendrye and his sons traveled through the upper Missouri River region. They buried a lead plate engraved with their names on a ridge overlooking the confluence of the Bad and Missouri Rivers. The elder de la Verendrye was later killed in a conflict with some Lakota. But his party's presence in the region was the beginning of European exploration and encroachment onto the northern Plains.

The de la Verendrye party had firearms and were not bashful about demonstrating the power and capability of their weapon-ry to the native inhabitants they met. The firearms were their balance of power. While the Lakota, or other tribes, were not afraid of the Frenchmen individually, they were afraid of the firearms.

As European incursions onto the northern Plains increased, the Lakota and others began to realize that the newcomers were an ambiguous anomaly.

The Europeans had knives made of iron and cooked food in iron kettles. They started fires by striking stone on iron. Among the Plains peoples knives were made of stone shaped and sharp-ened by percussion and pressure flaking. Cooking was done over open flames or in animal paunches filled with water and heated stones. For fire, starting embers were carefully maintained and taken from one camp to the next, or fires were started with devices such as a bow drill.

It was not so much that the first Europeans who came to the Plains brought new ideas or concepts, although that did happen to some extent. They brought improvements. An iron-bladed knife was more durable than a stone knife. An iron kettle could be used over and over again, and a flint and steel striker started fires faster than a bow drill.

The firearm, of course, was vastly different than the premiere weapon among the Plains tribes, the bow and arrow. White writers and historians unilaterally and ethnocentrically assume that the firearm was accepted and coveted by Indians everywhere. In their minds their ancestors had invented a superior weapon that replaced the bow and arrow in the blink of an eye. For the Lakota, it was not a simple issue of superior technology.

From the viewpoint of parity firearms were a necessity, because the lessons taught by the Ojibway were never to be forgotten. The Lakota understood that to be militarily prepared they had to be as well armed as their enemies.

While the firearm was effective at greater distances, until the introduction of repeating rifles in the mid-1860s, that was its only advantage. The muzzle-loading flintlocks, and later percussion rifles, were single shots. Elapsed time between shots varied from about thirty seconds to a minute. In that same amount of time, the average Lakota archer could nock, pull, and loose twelve to twenty arrows.

The Lakota realized that firearms in the hands of as many fighting men as possible would be an effective defense, and certainly a deterrent, against similarly armed enemies. The argument, therefore, was not against the practicality of having and using firearms. Any concern and initial hesitation was over what the firearm represented.

Within the societal structures of the Plains tribes, the adult male had definite roles and responsibilities. As the hunter he provided food and materials for shelter and clothing; as the fighting man he was the protector of home, family, community, and nation. During the course of his life he could also be a husband, father, grandfather, teacher, leader, seer, advisor, healer, storyteller, and role model. In order to fulfill his roles and meet his responsibilities, it was necessary for him to be as far as the

Lakota were concerned—a *wica* or a complete man.

In the Lakota language the noun for man is *wicasa*, for boy it is *hoksila*, for young man it is *koskalaka*, and for old man it is *wicahcala*. The hunter is *wakuwa* or *wakul wicasa* and the fighting man is *zuya wicasa*. *Wica*, therefore, does have a different connotation. To be *wica*, a complete man, was the ultimate goal of every male.

Europeans and Euro-Americans who traveled into the northern Plains knew nothing about the structure and functioning of Plains societies. Even the few who had closer contact than most made ethnocentric judgments. Since they didn't speak the language of their hosts, the intangible aspects of customs could not be adequately explained. An unfortunate consequence was misinformation, which was regarded as fact.

For example, the Plains Indian male was often away from home and the women performed all the domestic chores related to running a household. The Indian male was labeled by white observers as disinterested in the rearing of children, lazy and above performing the most menial of chores, forcing his wife into a life of toil and drudgery. To the white observer it was not always clear that the male was away from home in order to fulfill his responsibilities as provider and protector. And the observer had no way of knowing, or understanding, that the care of the home was the exclusive domain of the female and intelligent Indian males did not step into it.

Warfare was a fact of life on the Plains. But for individual tribes or individual males it was not a constant day-in and day-out activity. Functioning as a fighting man was only part of the male responsibility. When it was necessary to fight, all able-bodied men so inclined went into combat. And in that arena men strove to prove their courage and leadership because it was a way to achieve social and political status. Being a good and courageous warrior was one step on the way to being a complete man.

Throughout his adult life the four virtues he endeavored to

learn and manifest were fortitude, generosity, courage, and wisdom. Not everyone could, but those who did were respected, revered, and honored. Some became legends.

A complete man was well equipped to cope with the realities of his world, not because of what he held in his hands but because of what was in his mind and his heart. Such a man didn't need a weapon to define him because a weapon couldn't give him what he already possessed: self-awareness and confidence. While weapons certainly enhanced his ability to provide for and protect his family and community, without them he was still a man. Furthermore, within him was the skill and ability to turn raw materials into weapons, and tools.

The firearm was initially a weapon of mystery to the Lakota. Its capability was evident, but the idea of a small lead ball propelled by exploding black powder ignited by a spark from flint and steel was not an operative concept within their reality.

They called it *mazawakan*, which meant "mysterious iron;" *maza* meaning "iron" and *wakan* meaning "having a mysterious quality." The English word closest in meaning to *wakan* is "holy," and, of course, the translation which became popular is "holy iron."

Mazawakan is a name and a description based on tangible and intangible properties. Components of wood and iron were the tangible, and, in the beginning, its workings were the intangible. Soon enough the Lakota learned how to load and fire the weapon and one part of the mystery fell by the wayside. But another mystery remained and perhaps was never fully unraveled: the mystery of what the *mazawakan* did to the mind and spirit of a man.

The bow and arrow, the lance, war club, knife, and even a simple rabbit stick were painstakingly hand-crafted. Each man was individually responsible for making his own weapons and the level of their performance and effectiveness depended on how well they were made and how skillfully they were used. So a man had a connection, an intimate association, with each weapon.

There was another connection. Like him, the components of his weapon came from the Earth. Ash trees for bow billets; sandbar willow stalks for arrow shafts; sinew from antelope, bison, and deer for bow string; feathers from ravens, geese, and turkeys; and points fashioned from chert and flint. There was no mystery about a weapon a man carried to the hunt or into battle. It was a part of him and he was a part of it. The same could not be said of a holy iron or *mazawakan*.

For the Lakota there was an ambiguity to the *mazawakan*. It was a powerful weapon that could kill at far longer ranges than the bow. That capability appealed to younger men. Older, wiser men, however, could see that it possessed another kind of power.

Human inclination is to accept and use anything—be it a tool, weapon, or an idea—that makes life easier. When that happens the old and outdated is discarded. When the holy iron appeared among the Lakota, the bow had been the premiere weapon, but the holy iron made hunting easier and seemed to be an addition to the arsenal of the fighting man.

The demise of the bow as a weapon of choice and practicality began with the arrival of the holy iron. But for all it offered it was also a threat to an ancient tradition, and the avowed purists among the older generation of Lakota males were quick to realize that. To be a complete man one had to walk a hard road, one had to face, experience, and endure difficulty. For it was difficulty and hardship which shaped the man, not the easy path. The holy iron pointed down a different path, a shortcut to status or the appearance of it and away from the difficult and formative path of being a complete man.

A hunter with a bow had to place himself within about forty yards of his prey, which was the effective range of his weapon. As a hunter in the field he was already proficient with his weapon. He had learned to track and stalk, drawing on the knowledge and experience of his mentors and spending countless days in the field in all kinds of weather, until he was at home in the forest or on the prairie. Furthermore he had prepared himself for the hunt practically as well as spiritually. The hunter smudged himself, his clothing, and his weapons with smoke from gray sage to cover his scent. He prayed for success. Just as importantly he prayed for forgiveness for the lives he was about to take.

The hunter with a holy iron didn't have to position himself as close to his prey. Killing was easier with the holy iron and he eventually began to regard his prey as nothing more than a resource to satisfy the human right to survival. Over time he lost respect for life because he thought that the weapon in his hands made him superior to every other living thing.

The holy iron probably arrived among the Lakota in the mid-eighteenth century. Eighty years later, by the 1830s, it was so highly coveted that a few young men were driven to murder to own it.

Trade with the whites or capturing one from an enemy were the only ways to acquire a holy iron. Whites wanted treated furs or buffalo hides and tongues in payment for trade rifles–muzzle-loaders manufactured especially for the Indian trade. About 1840 a few young Dakota men who did have firearms went after buffalo on the prairies just east of the Great Muddy River, in what is now central South Dakota. In a few short days they managed to kill several hundred to a thousand head. A few hides were taken but the tongue was cut out from every kill and the rest of the carcass was left to rot. To be sure the coyotes, wolves, buzzards, and insects feasted. But to the Lakota, Dakota, and Nakota people who learned of the incident, it was not hunting in any sense of the word. Traditional preparation had been ignored and the purpose of the killing was not to supply meat and hides for the needs of the people. It was simply to trade for holy irons. It was murder committed to gain individual, selfish gratification. Those young men were seeking the status and power they thought the holy iron could give them.

In the space of eighty years the holy iron was able to weaken ancient beliefs and traditions associated with hunting.

For the fighting man the result was similar. Warfare was a necessity at times. But it was also an opportunity to display bravery and leadership, and gain honor. With primitive weapons combatants had to fight close in. The battle was joined face-to-face and there was no denying that the enemy was human.

The ability to demonstrate bravery in battle was a high honor. To touch a living enemy in the midst of battle and, of course, to live to tell about it was one of the highest honors. Putting one's life at risk to rescue a wounded comrade or remove a fallen comrade from the battlefield were other high honors. Yet another was the vow and the deed of fighting to the death.

Victory was the ultimate objective in battle. Combat was a terrible proving ground because of the real threat of injury and death. To achieve honor on that ground was the goal of every warrior. Demonstrating bravery in the face of the enemy was preferable to killing him. Wounds and death did occur and many men believed that dying in the defense of one's people was the highest honor of all.

One side would usually disengage when the persistence and power of the other side were too much to counter effectively, at which point the winning side would also disengage because victory was not always measured in the number of enemy dead.

The holy iron in the hands of one side and not the other was certainly a deterrent. It frequently won an encounter without a shot being fired. There were also instances when it tipped the balance of power in favor of a usually less aggressive or smaller group.

The use of the holy iron as a weapon of war did not significantly change the fighting style of the Plains warrior, once opposing tribes acquired the weapon in fairly equal numbers. However, it eliminated the need and the tradition for close combat. Combatants could fire at one another from fifty yards or more. They became faceless. Such obvious changes in tactics did not diminish the need for effective combat leadership or courage under fire, but it was a subtle erosion of the warrior code of conduct, a code which required honor. In other words, there had to be civilized behavior even in the midst of one of the most uncivilized of human activities.

The holy iron was a weapon of attrition. The traditionalists who practiced the ancient philosophy of being *wica*, the complete man, knew it would be necessary to acquire the holy iron in the interest of self-defense. They also knew that it would weaken the essence of their tradition. The holy iron was an easy fix, a powerful weapon as well as a source of power for some.

There were those men, however, who regarded the holy iron for what it really was: a weapon, no more and no less. That it had nothing to do with being a man, or not being a man. Those individuals did not dispute the military significance of the weapon, but they kept it in perspective.

On September 6, 1877, one of the last of the *wica* was killed at Fort Robinson, Nebraska. Crazy Horse was stabbed by a soldier with a bayonet affixed to a rifle, a holy iron.

In this day when a holy iron is still instant gratification, when the worth of a man is sometimes measured by how powerful and expensive his hunting rifle is, circumstances cry out for the complete man, the complete person. The kind of person, man or woman, who knows his or her strengths and weaknesses, and capabilities and limitations. The kind of person who can keep victory and loss, achievements and setbacks, in perspective. The kind of person who understands that every experience, good or bad, is part of learning and growing. One who faces the world and solves problems with what is in his or her mind and heart, and not what is in the hand.

In a nation of two hundred seventy million people, millions of firearms are part and parcel of our culture, from television to movies to toy stores, from the home to the gun rack in the pickup truck. The manufacture and sale of firearms is a multi-billion-dollar industry annually in this country alone; a powerful sacred cow if there ever was one. But there is another statistic, another number we should not overlook. Thousands of children are injured or killed by firearms every year in this country—fourteen a day.

The firearm is an inanimate object. It cannot load, aim, and fire. But there is something to be said for the name given to it by the Lakota who saw it for the first time some two hundred years ago: *mazawakan* or "mysterious iron," "holy iron."

To those who named it initially, it was a mystery. They also realized that it had a quality that had nothing to do with its functional ability. It offered an illusion of power. And that will always be the lure of the holy iron.

Other Museum of New Mexico Books by Joseph Marshall III

Winter of the Holy Iron
ISBN 978-089013-517-4

In the winter of 1750, a holy iron (flintlock rifle) and two Frenchmen are thrust into the lives of the Wolf Trail band of the Sicangu Lakota. Few white men have previously ventured onto the plains west of the Great Muddy (Missouri) River. Whirlwind, a war chief, finds his people divided in their feelings about the intrusion of the holy iron into their lives and what it could mean to their future.

On Behalf of the Wolf and the First Peoples
foreword by Roger Welsch
ISBN 978-089013-516-7

In this collection of essays, Joseph Marshall III gives opinions on both historical and contemporary topics from the perspective of a Native American. He addresses issues common to contemporary Native Americans, such as the definition of "Indian art" and the stereotypical Indian portrayed in film.